Cotswolds 2

England's Most Enchanting Destination

Walks, Attractions, Food, Accommodations and Everything In Between for Planning Your Perfect Cotswolds Adventure

Henry Winston

Map of Cotswolds

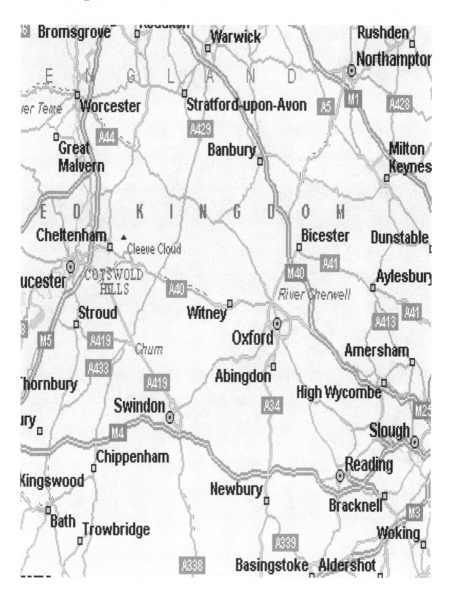

Cotswolds Travel Guide 2024

Enjoy your Stay in Cotswolds

TABLE OF CONTENTS

Contents

Introduction

Location and Overview

Nestled in the heart of England, the Cotswolds region is the quintessential vision of rural British countryside. Spanning nearly 800 square miles across five counties, it comprises gentle rolling hills, sleepy villages clad in honey-colored limestone, stately gardens, market towns and sweeping green landscapes as far as the eye can see. The rural, picturesque scenery looks as if it were lifted straight from the pages of a Victorian-era novel.

Just a few hours from London, the Cotswolds offers visitors an easy escape to discover England's pastoral landscapes and heritage. As one of the country's official "Areas of Outstanding Natural Beauty" designated by the government to preserve the rich nature and culture of the region, the Cotswolds cradles century-old traditions. Thatched roof stone cottages house modern country pubs and inns, locally-sourced food prevails on menus, timeworn walking paths meander through the countryside, and community festivals celebrate seasons and timeless customs.

The Cotswolds derives cultural significance from its history as a center of wool production in England spanning over 700 years through the height of the Medieval era. Vast sheep farming across the Cotswolds' gentle slopes yielded mass exports of wool and cottages handcrafted textiles, bringing wealth and infamy to the region. Many towns and villages still maintain active weaving workshops today along with larger mills converted into retail stores for shoppers to bring home the trademark "Cotswolds wool" items.

Beyond the world-renowned wool, the legacy of Arts and Crafts movement also blossomed across the Cotswolds around the turn of the 20th century. Pioneers like designer William Morris and Sir Edwin Lutyens left enduring marks through perfectly preserved homes, gardens and decorative art that visitors still flock to. Quaint country gardens rambling with flowering vines, hand-etched glass found in pubs, and collections of crafts make exploring the storybook towns of the Cotswolds even more magical.

While the pace of life glides slowly through the countryside, popular market towns like Cirencester provide hubs of activity. Wander narrow lanes of stone cottages or stop at a roadside farm store stocked with local produce and goods before mingling with locals at the centuries-old markets. The architectural heritage endowed by the Romans also comes alive at sites like the intricate museum RPG\Chedworth Roman Villa.

Beyond the villages, the immense Blenheim Palace introduces the grandeur and nobility of the area with its sprawling grounds, magnificent state rooms and gardens designed by Capability Brown. Charming towns like Burton-on-the-Water with its photogenic 17th-century stone bridges and riverside provide endless opportunities for relaxing riverside walks between quirky independent shops, cafes, and historic sites.

The natural beauty of the Cotswolds also unveils year-round opportunities to enjoy England's great outdoors. The Cotswolds Area of Outstanding Natural Beauty maintains over 240,000 acres of open countryside ideal for rambling walks on networks like the 102-mile Cotswold Way. Pedal along quiet country roads to discover ruins, quaint churches and villages at your own pace. Or survey the emerald landscape from soaring hot air balloon rides.

At the end of a day unwinding through the countryside, hunker down in a rural inn, cozy Cotswolds cottage sleeping under beams, or unwind in a lounge chair on the manicured lawns of a country house hotel. Savor multi-course feasts paired with local ales, ciders and wine before the crackling of a fireplace.

With unspoiled nature, enduring heritage and pastoral landscapes that embody quintessential English countryside, the Cotswolds promises daydream journeys through rural villages, market heritage, stately homes, local cuisine and creative culture. Its honey-hued aesthetic lingers in the memory for years to come.

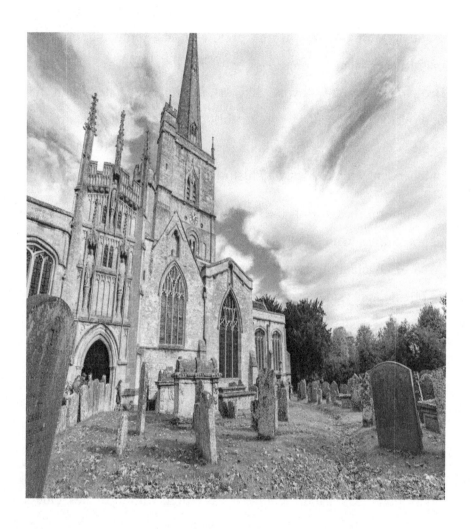

Chapter 1

Getting to the Cotswolds

- By Car

Driving offers one of the most convenient and flexible ways to explore the Cotswolds region. With its patchwork of winding country roads stitching together stone-walled villages, rural churches, crossroad markets and manor house hotels, traveling by car allows you to fully immerse in the countryside at your own pace.

The Cotswolds sits just a few hours northwest of London, making it an easy weekend road trip escape from the city. The region stretches across five counties, with Cheltenham on the west edge, Chipping Campden to the north, Swindon down south and Burford on the eastern border. Popular villages and attractions speckle across the 800 square miles in-between.

For those coming from London, the drive time averages around 2.5 hours depending on your starting point. Travelers can anticipate spending:

2 hours from Central London neighborhoods like Westminster or Camden Town

2.5 hours from West London hubs like Hammersmith or Chiswick

3 hours from Southeast London including Greenwich or Canary Wharf

The most direct route from London is to take the M40 motorway heading northwest out of the city towards Oxford through the heart of the Cotswolds. This takes you towards the eastern side of the region. Key towns and junctions along the M40 include High Wycombe, Oxford, Chipping Norton, Moreton-in-Marsh and Burford.

Driving west from London via the M4, you can access the southwestern portion of the Cotswolds. Towns along or just off the M4 include Reading, Swindon, Chippenham, Bath and Bristol. Popular southern Cotswolds destinations like Castle Combe, Lacock, Tetbury and Chavenage House reside in this direction.

General tips for navigating the Cotswolds by car:

Use GPS navigation to chart driving times and routes between villages. Cell service can be spotty in rural areas. Download offline maps and data to be prepared.

The M4 and M40 motorways allow you to quickly transit across or into the Cotswolds. But most towns and attractions require exiting onto local country roads, like those with B, C or unmarked road classifications.

Roads twist, turn and cross over each other with endless intersections of small villages. Give yourself ample time to traverse short direct distances.

Parking areas in popular market towns may fill up quick on weekends and bank holidays. Have back-up options ready in your navigation.

In some villages, roads remain small, fiercely winding and edged with tight stone buildings. Confident driving and maneuverability serves well.

While the motorways deliver convenience for reaching or crossing the region, embracing meandering backroads lets you soak up quintessential villagescapes. Stop to photograph half-timbered buildings smothered in ivy or colorful gardens exploding over Cotswold stone walls. Chat with a local farmer bumped into along an old drovers' road while taking in panoramic views of rolling green hills dotted with sheep. Or pull over at an enticing country pub or restaurant when hunger strikes.

With England's speed limits ranging 20-60 mph on average through the Cotswolds (besides select dual carriageways), tooling through the countryside by car provides a scenic way to watch rural life unfold. The relaxed pace also means you can casually stop as inspiration strikes without adding overly long to your journey.

While summer promises long sunny days ideal for top-down driving, fall showcases vibrant foliage and cozy venues full of crackling fireplaces. Wintertime brings holiday cheer to villages and twinkling lights draped around ancient buildings, churches and market squares. Crisp, foggy mornings give way to reveal stone homes encapsulated in snowdrifts.

With so much to uncover down winding lanes that crisscross the idyllic country landscape, driving lets you customize and spontaneously enhance your adventures through the Cotswolds. Stroll through hidden church cemeteries glowing in golden hour. Pop into quirky museums or galleries along your route. Squeeze in one more heritage garden or imposing manor house as afternoon light fades. Or chase another epic sunset vista spotted down an unnamed road.

With your own set of wheels, immerse yourself in all corners of the Cotswolds no matter what the season or allures you discover along your charming country drives.

- By Train

With an extensive rail network connecting directly into the Cotswolds, arriving by train makes for convenient, scenic transport without the hassle of driving. Railway lines cortege through the heart of the area's quintessential stone villages, sweeping valleys and market towns. From the ease of public transportation stretching from London and across England, trains unveil goods for both quick country getaways or longer holidays unwinding deep in the Cotswolds countryside.

Direct trains from London Paddington station can have you nestled into the picturesque Cotswolds landscape within 2 hours thanks to speedy connections averaging 80-100 mph. Key stops granting access points include:

- Moreton-in-Marsh – 1 3/4 hours from London
- Charlbury or Kingham – 2 hours
- Kemble – 1 3/4 hours
- Cheltenham Spa – 2 1/4 hours

Moreton-in-Marsh rests on the western Cotswolds line, operated by Great Western Railway with regular services to and from London, Reading, Oxford, Worcester and Hereford. The station resides just 3 miles from Stow-on-the-Wold and within easy reach of Chipping Campden, Broadway and Bourton-on-the-Water. Visitors can connect to local buses at the station.

Towards the northern part of the Cotswolds, Charlbury and Kingham stations offer gateways to idyllic towns and villages like Chipping Norton, Woodstock and Long Compton thanks to their Cotswolds Line operated by Great Western Railway. Ride in style aboard the antique Cotswolds Explorer heritage train in summer.

In the south, Kemble station provides the fastest access towards Cirencester, Fairford, Tetbury and Malmesbury, while Cheltenham Spa station sits just over 2 hours from London with connections across the southern Cotswolds.

Key tips for taking the train:

Booking in advance, even just a few days, can secure cheaper fares vs buying last minute tickets. Make reservations online via National Rail's website.

Trains run very frequently from London – up to every 30 minutes during commuter times and around every 1-2 hours otherwise throughout the day.

Transit options like the bus, local taxis or rental cars are available at Cotswolds stations but service frequency varies. Research connections ahead to your village.

Coming from northern England cities like Manchester or York, make transfers in Birmingham to reach stations like Moreton-in-Marsh.

Keep luggage minimal if needing to connect via buses or taxis. Storage lockers are available at select larger stations.

Download offline rail apps and maps ahead to stay on track with schedules, platforms and transit options while service is limited.

Once you arrive into a Cotswolds station, quintessential market towns and villages thrive just a short ride away ready to enchant through and through. Moreton-in-Marsh dazzles visitors with its weekly Tuesday open-air market in the town's bustling center lined with upscale boutiques, galleries, cafes and outdoor supply shops. Travel a few miles north to lose yourself in famous gems like Broadway or Snowshill.

Stow-on-the-Wold charms with its ancient market square, antique dealers and cozy local eateries full of character and hearty food. Nearby Bourton-on-the-Water delights with the River Windrush flowing under quaint pedestrian stone bridges in the town center. Bibury steals hearts with row upon row of honey-stone weavers' cottages set against the Coln river.

With rail stations continuing to expand across the central Cotswolds region, the ease of train transport unlocks doors to

English countryside reveries filled with wool merchants' mansions, imposing manor houses, immaculate gardens and mile after mile of footpaths traversing forests and farmland.

Check timetables to plot afternoon escapes, long weekend adventures or even week-long sojourns breathing in the fresh rural air. From the vantage point of a train window, watch how the landscapes transform from the bustling city streets of London to sheep dotted green hillsides and mazes of ancient stone walls blanketed in moss. Lose track of time strolling through quiet villages, cozy market halls and living heritage beneath age-old oak trees before returning home rested, recharged and inspired.

- By Bus

Crisscrossing through quaint villages and market towns, local buses in the Cotswolds offer an easy way to traverse the winding country roads and explore pastoral landscapes. While not as quick as traveling by car or train, buses provide a more affordable option to embrace the scenic journey through the countryside.

Connecting to major hubs around the Cotswolds, buses unlock transport deep into the honey-colored villages and stone cottages that look lifted straight from the pages of a storybook. Local lines including Pulhams Coaches, Johnsons Excelbus, Stagecoach,

Swanbrook, Cotswold Green and Marchants bring you close to famous gems like Bourton-on-the-Water, Stow-on-the Wold, Chipping Campden, Cirencester, Tetbury and Burford.

Key routes stretch from larger stations and towns into the countryside including:

- Moreton-in-Marsh to Stow-on-the-Wold, Bourton-on-the-Water and Chipping Campden
- Cheltenham to Bourton-on-the-Water, Northleach and Cirencester
- Cirencester to Tetbury, Malmesbury and Westonbirt Arboretum
- Gloucester to Painswick, Stroud and Woodchester Mansion
- Oxford to Woodstock, Charlbury and Chipping Norton

While most villages have some bus service, frequency ranges from every 30 minutes to only a few times per day. It's imperative to check updated schedules and plan connections in advance via apps or websites like Traveline Transit Planner.

Some key tips for riding buses:

Utilize larger hubs like Moreton-in-Marsh or Cheltenham to transfer onto local village routes.

Know exact change is required as drivers generally don't make change.

Check for route exceptions on Sundays and bank holidays when service is reduced.

Download offline maps and bus apps to stay on track since cell and WiFi service is limited.

Bus stops are marked but can be harder to spot in rural areas. Pay attention or risk missing your stop!

While bus journeys sacrifice efficiency for immersion into the countryside, rolling through little-known hamlets and landmarks grants a local experience. Watch shepherds herd sheep and farmers bail hay just outside the windows. Gaze up close at aged stone manor houses and cottages draped in vines and colorful gardens not visible from major motorways.

Connect beyond the popular sightseeing circuit through extended routes like Swanbrook's #812 bus called "Bats and Bells." Riding from Northleach to Bourton-on-the-Water the route winds through sleepy villages and fishing hamlets with potential stops at secluded Gothic churches and points of historic interest for those intrigued by bells and bat ecology.

Crisscrossing through the unsung western villages, Pulhams Coach Routes #853 and #854 link Tetbury to Malmesbury and hook north to picturesque Beverston Castle. Or try Marchants Belt & Braces route running between the North Cotswolds hills from Chipping Campden to Ebrington looping Burton-on-the-Water and Moreton-in-the-Marsh.

While limited in some respects, embracing the pace of local buses lets you mingle with locals commuting to work or running errands. Chat in line with village neighbors about the best regional restaurants or hidden heritage sites off the well-trodden tourist track.

Trading convenience for backroad revelations pays dividends through humbler perspectives of Cotswolds life. Glimpse sheepdog trials unfolding beyond stone fences. Survey stoic medieval church towers soaring over fairy tale stone cottages and inns bedecked with climbing roses and wisteria. Discover roadside farm shops brimming with local jams, cheeses and baked treats to sample along your journey.

By bus or by foot once you disembark, the Cotswolds offers endless adventures down each winding lane. Spend the day on mile after mile of footpaths to encounter soaring Abbey ruins, verdant gardens, trout filled streams under creaking willow trees and stalwart castles with epic histories. The transportation may be slower to savor the ride, but immersive experiences await at every uncharted turn.

- By Air

With an international airport just outside the Cotswolds in Bristol, flights offer the speediest gateway from destinations across the UK and abroad into England's treasured countryside. Additional regional airports pepper the outskirts of the Cotswolds, enabling air travel to launch memorable getaways wandering through postcard-worthy villages, imposing stately manors and the nostalgic English pastoral landscapes.

Just a 40 minute drive due south of Bristol lays Bath, marking the Cotswolds southwestern edge. The UNESCO World Heritage Site renown for its elegant Georgian architecture and Roman baths serves as a perfect pairing for extended stays. Travel east from Bristol Airport another hour to uncover the resplendent villages and lively market towns nestled in the North Cotswolds.

Bristol Airport receives regular direct flights from London, major UK cities and popular European destinations like Paris, Amsterdam and Dublin on carriers like KLM, Air France, Aer Lingus and Eurowings. Long-haul routes also connect travelers from New York City, Dubai, Doha and Toronto. Major airlines operate services within the UK through carriers like British Airways, Flybe, EasyJet and Ryanair.

In under 2 hours shuttle services and taxis efficiently transport visitors into landmark villages and towns across the central and southern Cotswolds like Tetbury, Malmesbury, Cirencester and Painswick straight from the airport doors.

Travelers looking to explore the north and east sections of the Cotswolds can consider flying into Birmingham Airport just under 2 hours car drive from gems like Chipping Campden, Broadway, Stow-on-the-Wold and Bourton-on-the Water. Trains also connect Birmingham Airport directly to Moreton-in-Marsh station in under 2 hours.

Birmingham receives a broad range international and domestic flight options as England's third busiest airport with leading carriers like Lufthansa, KLM Air France, Qatar Airways, Singapore Air and United Airlines. Regional budget airlines connect major UK cities into Birmingham on quick short-hop routes.

Additional airports on the periphery of the Cotswolds to consider include:

- Heathrow Airport – Under 2 hours drive to Burford, Fairford and Lechlade in the Southern Cotswolds
- London Luton Airport – 1 1/2 hour shuttle/drive to Chipping Campden and the central Cotswolds

- London Stansted Airport – Direct National Express shuttle route to Cheltenham, under 3 hours total

Upon arrival into the Cotswolds, hidden storybook gems entice exploration by rental cars, pre-booked shuttles or local taxis. Base yourself at a traditional coaching inn dotted for centuries along the old mail and trade routes through the region. Sip afternoon tea by crackling fires before heading into the countryside to uncover thriving market towns established in the Middle Ages.

Meander through epic gardens landscaped with pin straight cedar avenues, dazzling pergolas in perpetual bloom, secret grottos and follies from England's Golden Age of gardening. Hike along the Cotswold Way to survey breathtaking vistas over the Severn River Valley from Cleeve Hill and Broadway Tower.

Reflect on the Cotswolds significance amidst unspoiled nature while wandering through infamous Arts & Crafts heritage homes like Kelmscott Manor and Rodmarton Manor. Marvel at contemporary interior design fused into historic dwellings against backdrops of hills dotted with grazing sheep, golden wheat fields and lush green forests.

The ease of arrivals by air followed by drives through the sprawling countryside presents the perfect balance of modern transport and escaping into England's nostalgic pastoral landscapes. Find your own enchanting country abode to settle into for a week with cozy fireplaces, four poster beds with fluffy duvets to recharge energy amidst your blissful country ramblings.

With convenient airports granting swift access to and from the UK and Europe into the beauty of the Cotswolds, arrive refreshed, revitalized and ready to unlock year-round charms. Whether escaping the crowds for a winter holiday filled with bracing countryside walks or enjoying long summer days drenched in golden light perfect for al fresco dining, flights deliver convenient gateways to unlocking this magical countryside that lingers long after departing in your memory.

Chapter 2

Exploring the Cotswolds

- Bourton-on-the-Water

Situated in the heart of the Cotswolds region, Bourton-on-the-Water enchants visitors with quintessential English village charm. Often nicknamed the "Venice of the Cotswolds" thanks to the quintet of arched stone bridges traversing the River Windrush flowing through town, Bourton delivers picturesque scenery down every lane and street.

The Idyllic village spans just one mile from end to end but overflows with attractions, shops, cafes and historic sites to delight travelers of all ages. Bourton's central location makes it an ideal base with close proximity to signature Cotswolds towns and villages like Stow-on-the-Wold, Moreton-in-Marsh and Lower Slaughter.

Get your initial glimpse of Bourton's scenic bridges, riverside cottages and old stone walls while strolling along the one-mile village loop. Spanning both banks of the shallow River Windrush, quaint stone walkways crossing the water connect the two sides of town. Duck underneath small pedestrian footbridges and spy trout swimming in the clear water.

The scenic dykes were initially constructed in the 17th century by wealthy wool merchant William Clissold to help clean and power his nearby mill. Today, Bourton's bridges remain the iconic focal point where visitors gather for photos and views of ducks placidly floating by the waterwheel.

Wander into Bourton's compact but lively town center to discover an array of independent shops, tea rooms and cafes thriving within historic stone buildings. Peruse Cotswolds crafts like woodworking, ceramics and textiles at shops like the Cotswold Craft Centre. Source local gourmet goods and regional flavors from the Cotswold Cheese Co. Delight in homemade fudge and whimsical sweets at the Old Sweet Shop.

No visit to Bourton Is complete without indulging in a classic afternoon cream tea. Cozy up in the Rose Tree Restaurant's garden with delicate finger sandwiches, scones slathered in jam and whipped cream and a pot of fragrant tea. Or indulge in the Rose Tree's high tea at the end of a day filled with village explorations.

The Model Village gives you an aerial view of Bourton in miniature. Painstakingly created over decades to recreate the village at $1/9^{th}$ scale, it provides a chance to see historic buildings up close. The adjoining Model Railway also impresses with multiple model train lines chugging through tiny stations and villages.

Bourton's most famous attraction, however, is the Cotswold Motoring Museum. Home to one of the most extensive collections of vintage cars in England, it displays over 30 unique vehicles from 1906 to the 1980s. Don't miss the Mini Cooper family made famous in "The Italian Job" film from 1969.

Beyond the central village, ramble along the scenic footpaths bordering sweeping meadows leading to the upper and lower Slaughter villages less than 2 miles away. Or walk along the riverbanks through the Water Meadows park dotted with weeping willows. Reflect on Bourton's heritage at the parish church of St. Lawrence, parts of which date back to the 12th century on a site occupied for over 1,000 years.

After an action-packed day, unwind over dinner at The Croft, a 17th century coaching inn dishing up seasonal flavors showcasing locally-sourced produce. Sip a pint of the Cotswolds' famous local ales at The Old Manse Hotel's cozy pub/garden originally dating from the 15th century.

For overnight stays choose from countryside inns, boutique hotels and historic cottages. Bourton House Canal Guest Cottages offer contemporary facilities within a converted mill and stables next to a restored canal basin. Barnsley House provides indulgent country manor service and luxurious gardens originally designed by Rosemary Verey.

With endless opportunities to embrace quintessential Cotswolds heritage set against the lush natural beauty of the winding River Windrush, Bourton-on-the-Water makes an unforgettable base to call home during stays in the English countryside.

- Bibury

Renowned as one of England's most beautiful villages, Bibury encapsulates the essence of Cotswolds charm. Located in the heart of the North Cotswolds, about 9 miles from Cirencester, Bibury has captivated visitors for centuries with its honey-colored stone cottages, charming arched bridges over the River Coln, and unspoiled natural beauty.

Once described by 19th century designer William Morris as "the most beautiful village in England," the enchanting settlement has preserved its history and scenery. Take a peaceful stroll along the Trout Farm Walk beside the River Coln to absorb sights like the row of iconic 17th century weavers' cottages framed by bright flowers and swaying trees.

The Arlington Row cottages were originally built in 1380 as a monastic wool store before being converted into weavers' homes in the 1600s. The symmetrical cottages are one of England's most photographed spectacles. Capture your own postcard-worthy shot of the 17th century cottages glowing in the soft Cotswolds light.

Peer inside the cottages to glimpse how silk and wool weavers lived in this idyllic riverside setting for centuries. Spare a moment to appreciate the efforts to conserve these historic places by the National Trust and English Heritage.

Wander beyond Arlington Row through winding lanes revealing stone houses draped in wisteria and roses that look plucked from fairy tales. Discover the historic Church of St. Mary set on the site of a Saxon church dating to 680 AD. Bibury Court, a 17th-century house and gardens by architect Sir Christopher Wren also captures history from the English Civil War era.

The River Coln winding through the heart of the village provides delightful opportunities for riverside walks past trout farms, rack isles, and water meadows. Hunker down on the grassy banks with a picnic lunch watching anglers cast their lines and ducks float by. The wooded walk between Bibury and the neighboring village of Coln St. Aldwyns offers serene gardens and historic stone homes to admire.

Back in the village center, stroll around the criss-cross of quaint streets lined with arts and craft shops selling pottery, books, souvenirs and antiques. Stop for afternoon tea and homemade cakes at one of Bibury's tearooms and cafes housed in antique buildings brimming with English charm.

The 17th century Swan Hotel provides cozy Cotswolds accommodation steeped in history. Sip a cider at the Swan's antique oak bar or dine on traditional dishes like shepherd's pie or fish and chips using locally-sourced ingredients. The hotel's location next to the River Coln makes a beautiful base.

Visitors also flock to the historic Trout Farm. First used during medieval times by monks to rear fish, the working trout farm today has an on-site restaurant, fishing spots and outdoor seating among the river and willow trees. Try the smoked trout or trout pate tasting platter showcasing the fresh local fish.

Beyond its iconic scenery along Arlington Row, Bibury holds countless photogenic vantage points from the Saxon Church graveyard overlooking the stone cottages to the 17th century bridge across the glittering River Coln. Capture the area's unspoiled natural beauty in all seasons from snow dusted cottages in winter to floral blooms in spring.

With less than 500 residents, Bibury keeps a quiet, tranquil ambience even amongst its popularity. Embrace the slow Cotswolds pace while wandering around landmarks frozen in time for generations. Relax by the soothing flow of the River Coln and breathe in the fresh country air before cozying up for a traditional pub dinner or good night's rest at a local cottage or inn.

It's easy to see why Bibury charmed the likes of William Morris centuries ago. With its captivating blend of scenic nature, fascinating heritage and village idyll, Bibury remains one of England's most beautiful corners today, best appreciated through leisurely wanderings.

- Broadway

Known as the "Jewel of the Cotswolds", Broadway is a postcard-perfect English village located in the northeastern region of the Cotswolds. Situated at the foot of the western Cotswold escarpment, Broadway captivates visitors with its wide main street lined with upscale boutiques, art galleries, restaurants and cafés. The village's honey-colored limestone buildings date as far back as the 16th century.

Take a scenic stroll along The Green, Broadway's impressively broad main street bordered by antique lamp posts, quaint storefronts and limestone cottages overflowing with colorful flower boxes. The village was historically a major coaching stop on the route from Worcester to London, hence the wide street to accommodate busy thoroughfare.

Today, Broadway retains its charm as cars and coaches have given way to pedestrians enjoying the cafés, art galleries, boutiques and museum along the main road. Pop into Broadway's traditional pubs like The Swan, The Crown and Trumpet Inn for a pint of local Donnington Ale and a ploughman's lunch.

Don't miss Broadway Tower set atop the escarpment just one mile south of the village, providing panoramic views over the Vale of Evesham. Built in 1799 as a picturesque folly in the Gothic Revival style, the landmark 65-foot tower can be seen from miles away. Climb to the top for scenic views of the patchwork fields rolling into the distance. The grounds also feature a nuclear bunker and Cold War museum.

Broadway boasts both the National Trust's Snowshill Manor and Hidcote Manor Garden just short drives away, ideal for exploring the aristocratic life in the Cotswolds' stately homes coupled with masterpiece gardens. At Snowshill, wander through the cottage with its amazing collection of over 22,000 objects amassed by eccentric collector Charles Paget Wade.

Just two miles north of Broadway lies Chipping Campden, another famous Cotswold village brimming with remarkable architecture spanning over 600 years. Walk the 2 mile footpath between the villages, traversing rolling green hills dotted with sheep and traversing charming hamlet of Wickhamford.

Back in Broadway, browse the selection of independent shops selling artisan crafts, jewelry, clothes and homewares. Broadway Deli fills its shelves with great local produce, while Broadway Station serves as a quaint bookstore and café. Schedule your visit to coincide with Broadway's Farmers Market held the first Saturday of each month showcasing food producers and craftspeople.

Broadway offers a great range of traditional pubs, bistros, cafes and fine dining restaurants to satisfy any palate. The Swan serves upscale gastropub fare in a 15th century building with open fires. The Coach and Horses provides creative seasonal dishes and one of Broadway's best patios. Snag a table at Russell's for exceptional locally-sourced ingredients crafted into exquisite modern plates.

With one of the most beautiful high streets in England, Broadway offers a glimpse into timeless Cotswold life. Stroll the honey-hued limestone architecture of the high street before winding down quiet side lanes revealing chocolate box cottages and historic churches.

For accommodations choose from boutique hotels, cozy guest houses or well-appointed cottages just steps from the vibrant high street. The Lygon Arms, dating back to the 16th century, provides exceptional service and plush rooms. Broadway also makes a great base for exploring the surrounding Cotswold villages and attractions.

With its postcard-perfect streetscape, acclaimed restaurants and proximity to quintessential Cotswold delights, Broadway encapsulates the charm of the English countryside for an unforgettable village getaway.

- Chipping Campden

Situated in the northeastern Cotswolds, Chipping Campden epitomizes the idyllic English countryside with its golden limestone architecture, bustling Market Hall, imposing manor houses and immaculate gardens. Just 15 minutes drive from Broadway and under 10 miles from Stratford-upon-Avon, Chipping Campden makes an ideal base for exploring the North Cotswolds.

Begin at the narrow 14th century Market Hall standing proudly over Chipping Campden's High Street. One of the oldest market halls in England, its extravagant timber roof and arches have been meticulously preserved. Though no longer used for selling produce and goods, it remains at the heart of town life hosting special events.

Admire the impressive extent of Campden's historic architecture along the High Street and the adjoining Sheep Street. Look out for the Hick's Almshouse from the 17th century with its steep gabled roof and central bell turret. The Old Silk Mill, dating to the early 18th century, also highlights Chipping Campden's boom era as a prosperous silk and wool producing village.

Just north of town rises the imposing Jacobean manor house, Campden House, constructed in 1613 by affluent wool merchant Sir Baptist Hickes. Though mostly destroyed by fire in the English Civil War, the vast banquet hall with its extravagant plaster ceiling survives today for guided tours. The estate's remaining orangery, stables blocks and lodges provide insight into 17th century life.

Looming at the opposite end of town lays the 15th century St. James' Church, among the Cotswolds' finest wool churches. Spare time to stroll through the impressive churchyard landscaped with yew trees. Dating back over 1000 years, the site contains remarkable monumental tombs and carved gravestones worth admiring.

For delightful views over town, take the scenic walk up Dover's Hill to the Cotswold Voluntary Wardens Campden Tower. The 17th century Victorian gothic tower commemorates Queen Victoria's Golden Jubilee with panoramic vistas towards Chipping Campden's gabled roofs and the Slaughters valley.

Just two miles away near Broadway Tower, discover the extravagant Hidcote Manor Gardens owned by the National Trust. Explore the intricate garden rooms, vibrant flower borders and striking vistas across the landscape. Built in the 1920s, Hidcote represents one of England's finest examples of Arts & Crafts style gardens.

Back in Chipping Campden, indulge in laid-back Cotswolds dining at restaurants and pubs around the High Street. The Kings Hotel blends old world character and locally-sourced cuisine served indoors or in their charming garden terrace. For fresh bakes, grab breakfast at the scrumptious Badgers Hall Bakery tucked down Sheep Street.

Browse the boutiques and independent shops in town for local crafts, foodstuffs and souvenirs. Hart sells a chic edit of silver jewelry and luxury knitwear made in the British Isles. Fig Café dishes up creamy gelato, farm-fresh salads and flavorsome tarts in a sunlit garden café.

Whether admiring the Market Hall's architectural marvels, exploring grand estates and gardens or simply ambling the charming streets, Chipping Campden steeps visitors in history and quintessential English countryside. With historic inns, B&Bs and self-catering cottages, extend your North Cotswolds retreat in this remarkable market town.

Situated in the northern Cotswolds, Moreton-in-Marsh offers a lively market town experience amidst the tranquil English countryside. With its strategic location along the Fosse Way Roman road and the railway line, it serves as an excellent base for exploring the surrounding Cotswold villages and attractions.

Start your visit in Moreton's bustling town center focused around the impressive High Street lined with elegant 17th and 18th century buildings. The wide main street traces its origins back to Moreton's days as a coaching stop along the London to Worcester route.

Today, locals and visitors alike flock to Moreton's shops, galleries, pubs and eateries housed in historic stone buildings adorned with timber beams, brickwork and gabled Tudor facades. Pop into independent boutiques for women's fashions, homewares and gifts crafted by Cotswolds artisans.

Don't miss Moreton's largest draw – the lively Tuesday street market that has run for over 600 years. Rain or shine, over 200 vendors fill the High Street every Tuesday morning. Marvel at the bountiful displays of cheese, meats, fresh produce, breads and local crafts. Grab lunch from the hot food stalls or a snack from the cake and sweets stands.

Just off the High Street sits the oldest building in town – the 12th century St. David's Church. Don't miss the intricate medieval interior adorned with exquisite stained glass, hand-painted frescoes and a magnificent carved rood screen separating the nave from the chancel. The churchyard provides a tranquil spot for admiring Moreton's handsome surroundings.

Two miles northwest of town awaits Batsford Arboretum, a serene park brimming with exotic trees and shrubs spread over 56 acres of rolling hills. Meander through tranquility among flowering Japanese cherries, 15-foot tall Tibetan cherry trees and the largest private collection of magnolias in Britain. Seasonal blossoms provide color from March through November.

Visitors interested in immersing themselves into Cotswolds heritage can walk or drive the 2 miles northeast of town to charming Stow-on-the-Wold. Explore England's oldest cruel-free wool market filled with chic boutiques, artisan eateries and historic pubs. Climb to the top of St. Edward's Church tower for panoramic views of the Cotswold countryside.

Moreton-in-Marsh provides ideal access to many nearby Cotswolds gems. Lower and Upper Slaughter sit just 5 miles south amidst eye-catching scenery. Chipping Campden's remarkable architecture and gardens captivate 6 miles northeast. Bourton-on-the-Water's quaint walking bridges charm 7 miles west.

In the evening, dine on locally-sourced fare at chef proprietor restaurants like The White Hart Royal Hotel's smoked oak-paneled restaurant or The Horse and Groom's acclaimed fine dining. Or unwind with a flavorful pint at one of Moreton's six historic pubs like The Bell Inn, in operation since the 15th century.

With its central location in the Cotswolds, enticing shops and eateries housed in honey-colored limestone buildings, and the buzz of a traditional English market town, Moreton-in-Marsh offers a wonderful base for exploring the idyllic landscapes and villages of the North Cotswolds.

- Stow-on-the-Wold

Perched high atop an 800-foot hill deep in the heart of the North Cotswolds, Stow-on-the-Wold encapsulates the essence of a traditional English market town. With its vast tree-lined central square surrounded by historic pubs and antique shops, Stow provides a gateway to exploring the idyllic villages and scenery of the northern Cotswolds.

Begin your visit in Stow's bustling main square, the focal point of town. The large rectangular square gives insight into Stow's history as an important center for sheep trading from medieval times until the dawn of the railways. Stand at the base of the imposing 15th century cross situated in the center of the square, once used to direct sheep farmers to market days.

Wander the picturesque lanes branching off the central square like Sheep Street, Church Street and Talbot Court. Browse the boutiques and antique shops set inside iron-grey 17th century stone buildings with timbers and gabled roofs that have weathered the centuries. Duck into passages like Digbeth to uncover art galleries and craft workshops.

Don't miss the twice-weekly market held in the square every Thursday and Saturday. For over 700 years, local traders have gathered to sell fresh produce, artisanal foods, crafts and household goods against a backdrop of classic Cotswold architecture.

Just north of town sits St. Edwards Church, whose soaring 240-foot tower acts as a beacon across the countryside. Climb the tower's stone staircase to take in views of the ironstone rooftops and honey-hued buildings of Stow cascading down the hillside. Spare time to wander the churchyard and interior, which retains original Norman arches and pillars.

Two miles west awaits bourton-on-the-Water, dubbed the 'Venice of the Cotswolds' for its low stone bridges traversing the River Windrush that cuts through the village center. Meander along Bourton's riverbanks and pop into its cafes, shops and pubs housed in scenic stone buildings before looping back.

In the late afternoon, break for afternoon tea in Stow. Relax on The Porch House's outdoor terrace overlooking the square while indulging in tea, finger sandwiches and scrumptious scones. The 15th century building provides cozy, rustic digs steeped in history.

For dinner, indulge in traditional English cooking and local ales at The Bell Inn, which opened in the 1400s. Feast on familiar pub classics like fish and chips or pie and mash and sip a Cotswold brew at the Bell's original oak bar. With open fires and beamed ceilings, its cozy atmosphere evokes the charms of historic country life.

Stow offers accommodations options ranging from posh boutique hotels like The Wheatsheaf to family-run B&Bs and historic inns. The Manor House provides lavish rooms mixing classic style with modern comforts in a 14th century residence. Settle in for a restful night before new adventures among the enchanting villages and scenery of the Cotswolds.

With its sprawling market square, charming shops and proximity to top Cotswold sights, Stow-on-the-Wold encapsulates the spirit and beauty of the quintessential English village. Wander its historic lanes before setting off to explore more idyllic corners of the Cotswolds.

- Tetbury

Nestled in the southern Cotswolds not far from Westonbirt Arboretum, Tetbury charms visitors as a lively market town with roots dating back to the Anglo Saxons. With its constituent mix of medieval architecture, antiques shops, cozy pubs and proximity to Highgrove House, Tetbury makes a charming base for exploring the southern Cotswolds.

Start with a stroll down Tetbury's historic main thoroughfare called Long Street, a wide road dotted with open-air cafes perfect for people watching. Pop into stores housed inside the 17th and 18th century buildings that line the street, which meanders through town at an angle due to its curved medieval roots.

Browse the boutiques and antique shops displaying everything from vintage fashion and jewelry to reclaimed industrial furniture and elegant tableware. Stores like Tilly's Interiors and The Yellow House indulge antique lovers with rooms brimming with unique home décor spanning decades.

Each Wednesday and Saturday, Tetbury comes even more alive thanks to its bustling outdoor market held in the Market House right on Market Place. Vendors have gathered to sell their wares here since 1337. Today, over 100 traders set up on Market Days to peddle fresh produce, mouth-watering food stalls, household items, clothing and more against a backdrop of traditional town architecture.

No visit to Tetbury Is complete without indulging in tea and scones at The Gumstool Inn, a cozy 400-year-old inn oozing old world charm. Savor the heavenly homemade baked goods in the garden under the shade of an ancient lime tree or inside the exposed beam bar.

Tetbury's location in the southern Cotswolds countryside also makes it a great base for visits to nearby attractions. The magnificent Westonbirt Arboretum, home to over 15,000 trees and 2,500 different species, sits just 5 miles southwest of town. Highgrove House, the private residence and gardens of The Prince of Wales, gives select garden tours in summer by advance booking.

Within town, take in Tetbury's fascinating architecture spanning medieval, Georgian, Victorian and 20th century styles. The 12th century St Mary's Church exhibits exquisite stained glass and four 15th century pinnacles atop its iconic tower. Or admire the row of Weavers Cottages built in the late 1700s as worker homes for the wool and silk trade.

After a day exploring Tetbury's sights, indulge in relaxed dining at eateries around town. The Priory Inn dishes up elevated pub grub in a building originating as an 18th century farm. Menu highlights at Casa Sweet include stone-baked pizzas, grilled meats and fresh salads paired with local ales and ciders.

Accommodation choices in Tetbury range from luxurious country house hotels like Thyme and The Royal Oak Inn to cozy bed and breakfasts in historic abodes. Chavenage House provides an Elizabethan manor experience just 2 miles from Tetbury amidst 2,500 acres of oaks first planted in the 9th century.

With its thriving marketplace, honey-hued limestone cottages and proximity to southern Cotswolds delights, Tetbury makes an idyllic home base from which to explore the beauty, history and charm of this quintessential English market town.

Chapter 3

Must-See Attractions

- Sudeley Castle

Rising majestically amidst sweeping gardens and lush countryside just outside Winchcombe, Sudeley Castle encapsulates over a thousand years of English history within its turreted walls. From its origins in Anglo Saxon times to becoming the home and final resting place of Henry VIII's last wife Katherine Parr, Sudeley Castle dazzles visitors with royal splendor and exquisite grounds.

Begin exploring at the 10th century Saint Mary's Church situated on the castle grounds, one of the few surviving Anglo Saxon churches in the country. Then wander through the 15th century courtyard at the heart of the castle complex lined with half-timbered Tudor houses full of character. Don't miss seeing the grand banqueting hall where feasts and balls were once held by candlelight.

From the outside, marvel at the contrast of Sudeley's regal exterior featuring a long-reaching Jacobean façade painted creamy white against rambling roses along its façade. The east and south ranges built in the 1400s retain the castle's original defensive exterior with sturdy turreted towers and arrow slits.

Inside the castle, discover the splendor of the state rooms decked out in lavish textiles, ornate plasterwork, carved four-poster beds and intricate silver furnishings from the Victorian era. Stand in the breathtaking Long Room adorned in gold leaf detailing. It's easy to envision the glamor and conversations once held in these resplendent halls.

The private apartments of Henry VIII's sixth and last wife, Queen Katherine Parr, provide insight into 16th century royal living. Marvel at her Elizabethan bedding stitched by hand and exquisite embroidery. One highlight is the Queen's Garden she established that still bursts with colorful blooms today. Her tomb in the chapel remains part of the castle's allure.

Beyond the interior, Sudeley's widespread grounds impressed for over 1,200 years with features like the intricate Knot Garden planted with interlacing boxwood hedges in a Jacobean style. The lavish roses gardens bloom with over 200 varieties on display from June through September. Terraces, vines trailing the castle walls, and secret cottage gardens round out the grounds.

Families will love exploring the four different mazes and labyrinths woven artfully into the landscape. The largest is the tall yew hedge maze offering fun and mystery on its half-mile spiraling route. The Phoenician, Roman and Troy mazes each have different designs to investigate.

Younger visitors will enjoy the expansive adventure playground with a huge fortress and tower, zip lines, swings and climbing structures. Seasonal events like jousting shows, open-air cinema nights and exhibitions add to the magic. The charming tea room provides an ideal refueling stop during your explorations.

With an enchanting blend of history, architecture and nature over centuries of evolution, Sudeley Castle makes for an incredible day out. Visitors gain immense insight into English heritage while wandering the halls of kings and queens, strolling acres of formal gardens and simply absorbing the relaxed atmosphere away from bustling cities.

After a day transported back through the ages, extend your royal retreat by staying overnight in one of the castle's nine guest rooms. Choose from romantic four-poster bedrooms to family apartments in the lodges. Wake up and retrace your steps in the quiet stillness before the castle opens once more.

- Blenheim Palace

Situated just outside the Cotswolds in Woodstock, magnificent Blenheim Palace exemplifies English baroque architecture and aristocratic life as the birthplace of Sir Winston Churchill. From its imposing façade to over 2,000 acres of 'Capability' Brown landscaped grounds, Blenheim Palace dazzles visitors as one of England's grandest historical houses.

Construction on the palace began in 1705 after it was gifted by Queen Anne to John Churchill, the first Duke of Marlborough following his triumph at the Battle of Blenheim. Designed by Sir John Vanbrugh, the grandiose structure with its 187-foot high central clock tower took decades to complete, finally opening in 1733.

Today, Blenheim Palace remains the home of the 12th Duke of Marlborough and retains its glory as a UNESCO World Heritage Site. Walk the same extravagant halls where Sir Winston Churchill was born in 1874 and gain insight into English aristocracy through the centuries.

Beyond the palace itself, the grounds sweep extensively across parklands dotted with lakes designed by landscape architect Capability Brown in the 1760s. From the dramatic Long Water 2-mile stretch to the English Garden walls smothered in vines, the scenery provides context to the scale and grandeur.

Inside, ornate state rooms dazzle with tapestries, figurines, gilded ceilings and over 300 oil paintings. The saloon's trompe l'oeil murals trick the eye, while the library houses over 10,000 books beneath carved bookshelves and balconies. The opulent furnishings and décor reflect one of England's foremost private collections.

The historic staterooms also provide insight into Sir Winston Churchill's life during stays at his birthplace over his decades of public service. See the bedchamber where he worked during WWII and the compelling exhibition chronicling his life from childhood through his funeral in 1965.

Equally engrossing is the "Untold Story" exhibition highlighting the working life below stairs in the palace kitchens, game larder and staff quarters. Journey through the indoor riding school, learn about lavish feasts held inside the great hall and imagine the bustle behind scenes daily prepping food, cleaning and maintaining the palace.

For many visitors, the magnificent gardens and grounds are the highlight. Stroll through the lavender-filled Italian Garden adorned with fountains, symmetrical hedges and a cascade flanked by statues. The Secret Garden overflows with wisteria and roses surrounding a sparkling pool – a magical hideaway to wander.

Seasonal events also bring Blenheim Palace alive from its vivid flower shows to jousting tournaments on the lawn to Christmas décor transforming rooms into yuletide wonderlands. Concerts featuring headliners like Patti Smith to outdoor movies under the stars also take place annually in summer.

From its sheer scale and opulence to insight into aristocratic life shaped over centuries, Blenheim Palace makes for an unforgettable day out. It dazzles from every angle, whether appreciated from its imposing front façade or while strolling through its meticulously sculpted grounds. Visitors gain immense insight into English history within its spectacular confines.

- Warwick Castl

Rising majestically above the River Avon just north of Stratford-upon-Avon, Warwick Castle has dominated the landscape and British history for over 900 years. From its medieval towers and turreted ramparts to lush gardens and intriguing exhibits, Warwick Castle brings England's past vibrantly to life.

Perched on a sandstone bluff along a strong bend of the river, Warwick Castle was constructed in 1068 by William the Conqueror shortly after the Norman Conquest on the site of an earlier Saxon fortification. Over the centuries, it has transitioned from mighty medieval fortress to lavish family home for the Earls of Warwick to a Victorian Romantic revival to its current incarnation as a top visitor attraction bringing history to life.

Exploring the castle grounds, it's easy to imagine archers poised atop the lofty curtain walls and soldiers stationed in the gatehouses protecting the stronghold. Climb the towers and walkways for panoramic views over the river valley and gardens sprawled below. Discover dark dungeons and winding spiral staircases connecting the many rooms, towers and battlements.

Within the State Apartments and Great Hall, get insight into fine living and extravagant feasts held through the ages. Marvel at Europe's longest table in the Great Hall once used to host over 70 lavish banquets and events for invited guests. Don't miss special exhibits like the "Kingmaker" showcasing the Earls of Warwick's political influence.

The castle's 64 acres of grounds provide hours of leisurely discovery through ornate gardens, cascading fountains, grassy lawns and winding paths beneath shady trees. Relax while taking a falconry demonstration or get your heart pumping on the Knight's Village outdoor assault course navigating obstacles to conquer the tower.

A visit to Warwick isn't complete without exploring the medieval sword in hand exhibition displaying centuries of armoury and weapons. Handle swords, pikes, axes, bows and flintlock pistols to appreciate the weight and intricacies. Kids can try on a helmet, chainmail tunic or breastplate for an amusing photo.

Of course, the star attraction remains the castle itself with over 1,100 years of intriguing history practically seeping from its stone walls. Climb winding staircases to stand atop the parapets or pause in an arched window seat and ponder what castle life was like here during its heyday many moons ago.

Special events held annually like jousting tournaments, lavish medieval banquets, and evening ghost tours add to the theatricality and magic. Rooms decked out for Christmas offer a special chance to envision Tudor celebrations. Concerts and outdoor film screenings also take place on summer evenings within the atmospheric grounds.

Just two miles away lies Stratford-upon-Avon, Shakespeare's beloved hometown and burial site. Combining visits to both the magnificent medieval castle and the Bard's quaint timber-framed houses makes for an incredible pairing to experience England's history.

With its imposing turreted towers looming over the peaceful Avon valley, the scale and grandeur of Warwick Castle never fails to impress. Step back in time wandering its parapets and state rooms before relaxing in its gardens for a unique perspective on British heritage in one of England's finest castles.

- Broadway Tower

Soaring atop the escarpment on the western edge of the Cotswolds, Broadway Tower has been an iconic regional landmark since the late 18th century. Today, it continues to intrigue visitors as an architectural marvel offering unrivaled panoramic views across Gloucestershire, Worcestershire, Warwickshire and beyond.

Built in 1799 by Sir George Gilbert Scott for the 6th Earl of Coventry, Broadway Tower was envisioned as a picturesque pastoral retreat and folly, or ornamental structure built for enjoyment. Inspired by 12th century Norman design, the crenelated tower evokes a romanticized medieval aesthetic from its 65-foot height.

Visitors to Broadway Tower can appreciate Scott's vision while surveying the surrounding patchwork fields and villages that unfold for miles into the distance. On clear days, views span as far as Wales thanks to Broadway Tower's prime location atop the 1,024 feet high Cotswolds escarpment.

Inside the structure itself, interactive exhibits detail the tower's history and attractions of the broader Cotswolds region. Telescopes and observation points oriented on every side cater to sweeping vistas across counties from various angles. The tower's rooftop viewing platform delivers the most awe-inspiring 360-degree panorama.

The grounds surrounding Broadway Tower also offer much to discover for visitors. The 311-acre Broadway Tower Estate features woodlands carpeted in bluebells each spring, scenic walking trails traveling deep into the Cotswold countryside, and a quaint café for refueling during your explorations.

Families will delight in the adventure playground at the foot of the tower equipped with treehouses, tunnels, slides, swings and climbing structures to expend energy outdoors. The maze crafted from 2,500 yew plants interwoven across 1,500 feet also promises fun trying to find your way to the center and back out again.

Those intrigued by Cold War history will be fascinated touring the nuclear bunker buried over 50 feet underground near the tower. Built during the 1950s, the bunker space housed the Royal Observer Corps tasked with detecting nuclear explosions and fallout across the UK in the event of war.

Every corner of the estate provides opportunities to embrace natural beauty and Cotswolds heritage. Have a picnic while taking in vistas of grazing sheep and rolling green hills dotted with cozy villages. Follow winding footpaths through wildflower meadows and peaceful woodlands straight out of a Constable landscape painting.

Special events year-round add to the magic of Broadway Tower and its surroundings. Seasonal flower shows in spring and summer feature arrangements from local gardening groups. Outdoor theater performances set against the tower's iconic silhouette entertain on warm summer evenings. And the Christmas lights strung across the turreted structure sparkle wonderfully through the dark winter months.

Whether spotting landmarks from its heights, meandering scenic trails through its grounds or absorbing exhibits in its interior spaces, Broadway Tower encapsulates a unique blend of history, architecture and natural splendor. It's no wonder artists like J.M.W. Turner once flocked here to capture the majestic vistas overlooking the Cotswolds countryside. Visitors today can experience that same creative inspiration through sweeping views and pastoral charm just steps from charming Broadway village.

- Chedworth Roman Villa

Tucked away in the lush Cotswold countryside, Chedworth Roman Villa offers visitors a remarkable glimpse into life in Roman Britain nearly 2,000 years ago. This incredibly well-preserved villa complex stands as one of the most complete examples of elite Roman country life found anywhere in Britain.

Chedworth Villa was first discovered in 1864 by Victorian gamekeeper-turned-amateur-archaeologist, the Reverend Samuel Sheppard. As he dug into the site, the extent and excellent condition of the villa's mosaic floors, bathhouses, living quarters, and other structures began to reveal themselves. Further excavations over the following decades slowly uncovered the sprawling 8.5 acre (3.5 hectare) estate.

Today, visitors can wander through the various rooms, admiring the intricate mosaic floors that adorned living spaces, dining rooms, and bath complexes. The mosaics feature colorful geometric patterns as well as depictions of animals, plants, and classical mythology. One of the most famous is the "Orpheus Pavement" which shows the legendary Greek musician surrounded by birds, beasts, and trees, all drawn towards his enchanting melodies.

Particularly impressive at Chedworth are the remnants of the bathhouse complex. Fed by natural spring waters, the caldarium (hot room), tepidarium (warm room), and frigidarium (cold room) give great insight into the Roman's love of bathing and the important social rituals centered around their public baths. You can see the underfloor heating systems, plunge pools, and even the remains of painted wall plaster decorations.

As you wander the grounds outside, it's hard not to be struck by the countryside villa's bucolic setting. The Romans certainly had an eye for a picturesque natural landscape, situating the estate amongst gently rolling hills, lush woods, and the bubbling waters of the River Coln. You can almost imagine the elite Roman owners strolling the landscaped gardens, olive groves, and farmlands, enjoying fresh country air and relaxation away from the bustle of city life.

The excellent on-site museum does a wonderful job bringing the villa's history to life through recreated rooms, archeological finds, interactive exhibits and easily digestible information. You'll learn about the site's construction in the early 2nd century AD, its heyday in the late 3rd and 4th centuries, its abandonment around 360 AD, and the preservation beneath soil and grass that allowed so much to remain intact for modern visitors.

A visit to Chedworth Roman Villa makes for a fascinating day out. The site transports you back nearly two millennia, offering an unparalleled window into the luxurious country lifestyle enjoyed by elite Romans in ancient Britannia. With its incredible mosaics, bathhouses, domestic structures and idyllic natural setting, Chedworth gives you a true sense of "villa life" on a grand country estate. It's an unmissable highlight for anyone exploring the Cotswolds region's wealth of historic treasures.

For an up-close encounter with animals from around the world in a beautiful Cotswolds setting, look no further than the Cotswold Wildlife Park. Situated on over 160 acres of idyllic parklands and gardens, this zoo offers the chance to view hundreds of different species roaming through immersive, naturalistic enclosures.

As you enter through the main gates, you'll find yourself immediately immersed in the park's lush, landscaped grounds. Winding pathways meander through mature woodlands, flower gardens, lawns, and lakes – a perfect environment for both people and animals to explore. The park's layout and design make the most of the gently rolling Cotswold terrain and countryside scenery.

One of the first areas you'll encounter is the Cotswold Cats and Threatened Species section. Here you can see sleek cheetahs lounging in the sun, majestic snow leopards padding across rocky outcrops, and rare Amur leopards stalking through forested enclosures. These powerful felines are just a taste of the many threatened species you'll be able to observe up close at the park.

Continuing along the trails, you'll come across the huge Asian Plains area, home to Indian rhinos, Asiatic lions, and sloth bears among others. This massive habitat recreates the look and feel of the animals' native lands. Walk across a raised boardwalk while Asian elephants graze and play below. The rhinos in particular love to wallow and bathe in the large pools and mud wallows.

For primates galore, head to the primate area featuring squirrel monkeys, spider monkeys, ring-tailed lemurs, and Western Lowland gorillas. The gorilla kingdom offers an unbelievable opportunity to watch these powerful yet gentle giants interact and move about their forest-like habitat. With a bit of luck, you may even catch the famous silverback male gorilla putting on a display of chest-beating dominance.

Kids will absolutely love the park's Madagascar Walkthrough where they can wander beside free-roaming lemurs leaping from tree to tree around them. Be sure to check out the Reptile House as well, showcasing scaly snakes, lizards, and tortoises in naturalistic habitats.

One of the real highlights is the train safari, included with admission. This narrow-gauge railroad takes you on a 25-minute journey through the open, drive-through savannah areas of the park. From aboard the train, you'll have incredible views of roaming species like white rhinos, giraffes, zebras, antelope, camels, and more, all living together as they would in the wild.

Beyond just observing the animals, the park offers loads of interactive experiences as well. You can book animal encounters to go behind-the-scenes and get up close with species like meerkats, penguins, and lemurs. There are also daily keeper talks, animal feedings to watch, and seasonal activities like newborn animal viewings.

The Cotswold Wildlife Park makes for an incredibly fun yet educational day out for families, animal lovers, and anyone with an interest in conservation. The exhibits successfully recreate habitats and environments that allow the animals to live as naturally as possible while visitors get a front-row view from immersive trails and outlook points.

With its wonderful mix of exotic and endangered species, its lovingly designed park grounds, and its emphasis on presenting animals in natural-looking open enclosures, the Cotswold Wildlife Park is an absolute must for anyone visiting the area. It's entertaining and enlightening while also promoting the importance of protecting the world's wildlife. A true gem in the heart of the Cotswolds.

- Snowshill Manor and Garden

Hidden away down a long, winding lane in the heart of the Cotswolds lies the enchanting Snowshill Manor and Garden. This captivating 16th century manor house, owned by the National Trust, offers visitors far more than just another historic home to tour. It's a journey into the eccentric mind of one man and his boundless collection of curiosities and treasures.

Charles Wade was an exceptional man, to say the least. An artist, poet, architect, craftsman – his true passion was amassing an unbelievable array of objects and antiquities from around the world. In 1919, at the age of 54, Wade happened upon the semi-ruined Snowshill Manor and made it his life's mission to restore it as a home for his ever-growing collection.

As you approach the golden stone manor, you get your first glimpse into Wade's unique vision. The grounds are landscaped into a series of small, walled gardens, each with its own theme and character. You'll wander through the geometrically designed Quartermain Garden, the Tudor-style Samian Garden, the wooded Elemental Garden, and more surprises at every turn.

Stepping inside the manor's rooms is when you start to understand the true scope of Charles Wade's relentless collecting and creativity. Every inch of space in the dimly lit, atmospheric interiors is filled to bursting with objects gathered over his lifetime – an astounding 22,000 items in total.

Wade's interests ranged from the conventional to the bizarre. Antique furniture jostles for space alongside intricate wood carvings, Samurai armor, woodworker's tools, model ships, toys, voodoo masks, instruments, stuffed animals, and even a recreated Renaissance privy. You'll turn a corner to find the unexpected – a full-sized Vietnamese torah, Russian Orthodox iconostasis, or a large seventeenth century figurehead from a Dutch ship.

Each room has its own theme and featured pieces, all meticulously curated. Wade devoted decades to arranging and rearranging his possessions in creative and whimsical ways. One of the most impressive is the Painting Room, its walls completely covered in artworks in carved frames forming intricate, concentric patterns. Other standout rooms include the Tiger Room, lined in tiger fur from Amsterdam, and the Windmill Study with its miniature rotating windmill poking through the ceiling.

As you tour Snowshill Manor, you can't help but be struck by the boundless creativity and obsessive quirks of the collector who assembled it all. Charles Wade truly had an artistic genius for arrangement. He brought order and beauty to his overwhelming trove of acquisitions, no matter how humble or high-brow they might have been.

Your visit wouldn't be complete without wandering the scenic gardens and grounds that surround the manor. In addition to the intimate walled gardens, don't miss the vast kitchen garden which provided fruit, vegetables and herbs for the manor. Follow the woodland trails beside the mill pond and stream to discover follies, grottoes and even an "underground fantasy" featuring Sumerian carved figures.

After several hours roaming through Snowshill, you'll emerge amazed, perhaps a bit bewildered, but utterly enchanted. Charles

Wade's idiosyncratic creation, assembled with a true artist's eye and unbounded enthusiasm, must be experienced to be believed. Snowshill Manor is a Cotswolds gem that offers treasures, beauty, and surprises around every corner for the curious traveler to discover. It's a living embodiment of one man's unique and fervid vision that simply must be seen.

- Hidcote Manor Garden

Widely considered one of the most influential and important Arts and Crafts gardens in the world, Hidcote Manor Garden is an absolute must-see for any visitor to the Cotswolds. This breathtakingly beautiful series of outdoor "rooms" was the life's work of American expatriate Major Lawrence Johnston and stands today as his living masterpiece.

As you approach Hidcote along a tree-lined driveway, the first glimpse of the gardens comes when you spy the golden-hued 17th century manor house peeking over the hedges and topiaries. From the very start, you realize you are somewhere special, a place of meticulous planning and artistic vision.

The garden surrounds the manor on all sides, divided into a series of distinctly designed and themed enclosures. Major Johnston's genius was in linking these many intricate gardens and vistas through clever use of vistas, hedges, steps, and pathways to create a cohesive yet varied whole.

One of the most iconic areas is the White Garden, filled with an incredible tapestry of green and white plantings that billow over stone walls and paths. Hydrangeas, lilies, jasmine, and roses fill the air with their perfume. A serene circular pool reflects the clouds above.

Nearby, you'll discover the Old Garden, the first area planned by Johnston in 1905, with its pleached linden trees and geometric boxwood parterres. The Stilt Garden, with its raised paths and plantings, overlooks the Old Garden and surrounding countryside through archways in yew hedges.

A gravel path leads you through an opening in towering yew hedges to discover the Hidden Garden, a lush enclosure filled with exotic trees and plants in a naturalistic style. A series of linked pools run alongside, their tranquil waters reflecting the flowery borders.

From the Hidden Garden, you'll come to an intersection known as the Circus, which acts as the central hub connecting to radial paths and vistas through hedged alleys. These alleys, known as bathing sheds, offer focused views of specific plantings and focal points like stone ornaments.

The bathing sheds and hedged rooms culminate at the Maple Garden, one of Hidcote's largest enclosures and most impressive achievements. Here, Johnston created a perfect harmonious balance of trees, shrubs, and flowers surrounding a large central pool. It's a masterwork of thoughtful garden design achieving a sense of proportion, color, and delight.

Throughout Hidcote, the pilgrimage paths and hidden vistas continue to unfold, surprising you with new delights around every corner. Perhaps you'll stumble upon the secluded Wildflower Meadow, the Beech Circle, or the Bathing Terrace. A set of stone steps may lead down to an unexpected sunken garden. Ornamentation like stone basins, ornate gateways, and classically inspired pavilions add decorative flourishes.

One of the real pleasures of visiting Hidcote is seeing how Lawrence Johnston took inspiration from numerous garden styles and movements and fused them into his own unique creations. You'll find elements of English cottage gardens, Italianate formality, Oriental minimalism, and more. Everything is planned meticulously yet maintains an almost whimsical sense of discovery.

Today, the gardens are cared for by the National Trust and remain very true to Johnston's original designs and plants. Additional interpretation, signage, and written materials help visitors understand the vision, history, and plants that went into creating this internationally renowned garden.

A visit to Hidcote Manor Garden never fails to inspire awe and delight in anyone with an appreciation for gardens and nature. To slowly wander its labyrinth of hedged rooms, pools, and plantings is to be transported to a world of cloistured serenity, fragrant perfumes, and visual enchantment. Lawrence Johnston's consummate skills and artistry allow modern visitors to experience the same garden joy he so painstakingly and perfectly sculpted over decades. It's an absolute must for anyone with a passion for gardens or the simple pleasures of nature's beauty.

Hidden away down a long, winding lane near the picturesque Cotswold village of Chipping Campden lies the absolutely enchanting Kiftsgate Court Gardens. This series of interconnected gardens surrounding a historic manor house represents the life's work of not one, but three generations of passionate gardeners from the Muir family.

As you approach the main gardens, the first glimpse is of the iconic Kiftsgate Rose climbing over archways and stone buildings. This famous climbing rose, which can reach heights over 30 feet, was a chance hybrid first cultivated here in the early 20th century.

It sets the tone for the whimsical, romantic gardens you're about to discover.

One of the earliest and most acclaimed areas is the White Sunk Garden, created in the 1930s by Heather Muir. Descending stone steps lead you down into a lushly planted sunken garden with a classic Cotswold stone pavilion and lily pool at its center. Pathways meander between profusions of white-blooming plants and decorative topiary.

Nearby, Heather's daughter Diany continued the family's gardening legacy by creating a series of water gardens in the 1950s. A circuitous stream connects a chain of small ponds and rock gardens. Tiny bridges arch over trickling waterfalls and lush plantings cluster along the waterways. It's an area of supreme tranquility and natural beauty.

One of the loveliest areas is the Garden Terrace, with its flagstone paving and flower borders spilling over with roses and perennials. Here you can take in sweeping views across the Vale of Evesham to the Malvern Hills in the distance. Stone ornaments scattered throughout add decorative focal points.

From the Garden Terrace, steps lead down to discover a series of interlinking garden enclosures. Pass through tunnels of pleached hornbeams into areas like the Pear Tree Garden and the Rose

Circle, where flower beds surround a central stone basin. The Fuchsia Garden and Rock Garden are awash in colorful plantings.

Another highlight is exploring the dense Ladies' Wildflower Woodland. A maze of grass paths weave through towering oak, beech, and ash trees. In spring, carpets of wildflowers like bluebells and wood anenomes cover the ground. In autumn, this is one of the best places in the gardens to admire the fall foliage.

As you continue exploring, you'll discover hidden garden alcoves tucked away and plenty of places to sit and lose yourself in the peaceful surroundings. Stone seats encircle trees, wooden benches reside in secluded corners, and defined clearings offer spaces of tranquility.

The most recent additions are the Lower Gardens, masterminded by Graham Muir in the late 20th century. A classically inspired round pool fringed with box hedges and lavish plantings sits at the center of a large geometric parterre. Nearby, a new undulating Rill Garden features a long, narrow stream winding down a grassy slope between trees.

Throughout all areas of Kiftsgate, there is such a wonderful harmony achieved between structured garden elements and more naturalistic plantings. The gently sloping terrain is used masterfully, allowing for hidden vistas and a journey of garden discovery around each corner. Major garden structures like pavilions are always perfectly placed as focal points for the eye to rest upon.

One of the real joys is seeing how Kiftsgate has evolved over multiple generations while retaining a coherent overall vision. The Muir family have an expert understanding of form, color, and proportion. Their expressive, romantic style gives the gardens a dreamlike, almost fairytale-esque quality.

For any visitor with an interest in gardens, a trip to Kiftsgate is an absolute treat. The gardens welcome you in from the moment you first spy their iconic rose, beckoning you to slow down and savor nature's beauty. It's an oasis of tranquility where modern visitors can experience the culmination of decades of passionate gardening by a family devoted to creating outdoor spaces of incredible charm. Kiftsgate is sure to delight and inspire anyone who wanders along its paths.

Chapter 4

Outdoor Activities

- Walking and Hiking Trails

With its gently rolling hills, quiet countryside lanes, and network of well-trodden footpaths, the Cotswolds is an absolute paradise for walkers and hikers. Lacing through tiny villages of honey-colored stone, alongside babbling brooks, and across expansive farmlands and woodlands, the area's public walking trails offer some of the most scenic rambling in all of England.

For many visitors, the quintessential Cotswold walking experience is to set out on one of the many circular village trails that radiate from the region's postcard-perfect market towns and hamlets. These well-marked routes, usually between 3-6 miles in length, allow you to park your car and experience the surrounding countryside on foot, passing through fields, forests, and along ancient rights of way before returning to your starting point.

Two of the most popular circular routes are the Bourton-on-the-Water circular walk and the Stow-on-the-Wold circular walk. From Bourton, you'll wander along the meandering River

Windrush, traverse small valleys and countryside hamlets like Clapton and Little Rissington. The Stow walk takes in the sweeping landscapes of the Cotswold Hills and passes through quaint villages including Lower Swell with its photogenic cottages. Both of these relatively easy trails of around 4-5 miles provide the perfect taste of what Cotswold walking is all about.

For those looking to explore further afield over multiple days, an extraordinary network of long-distance hiking trails crisscrosses the entire region. You could easily spend a week or more traversing the Cotswold countryside from inn to inn along paths like the Cotswold Way National Trail, the Oxfordshire Way, or the Gloucestershire Way.

The crowning glory is the 102-mile Cotswold Way which winds in a giant arc through the region's most spectacular scenery and iconic villages. Following the western edge of the Cotswold escarpment, the trail takes you through pastoral valleys, over rolling hilltops offering incredible vistas, along shaded woodland trails, and past ancient sites and estates. Highlights include the stunning Broadway Tower, picturesque Painswick village, and the bohemian town of Stroud. With its ever-changing scenery, it's easy to see why the Cotswold Way has become one of Britain's most popular and beloved long-distance trails.

For an immersive and informative hiking experience, consider joining one of the many guided walks and hikes led by local experts and tour companies. Operators like Cotswolds Guided Walks provide a variety of itineraries, from half-day rambles to multi-day treks, led by knowledgeable guides. Not only will you experience the trails, but you'll gain insights into the region's rich history, culture, nature, and communities through the stories and information they share along the way.

Exploring the Cotswolds on foot, you'll be following in the footsteps of generations of wanderers who've discovered this sublime landscape at a walking pace. The area's dense network of public paths and trails were forged over centuries byossiers, farmers, and miners as they moved between villages and settlements. Taking to these routes today, you can still visit secluded churches, once-thriving market towns now frozen in time, and ancient archaeological sites that have survived for thousands of years.

One of the great pleasures of hiking in the Cotswolds is stumbling upon sights and scenes that embody the quintessential English countryside. A flower-lined brook flowing under a tiny stone bridge. A farmer's herd of sheep or cows grazing on a hillside. Dense woodlands with a maze of rootsy paths. Old field patterns created by miles of centuries-old stone walls. A village green surrounded by thatched cottages. These are the scenes that etch themselves into memory on a Cotswold walk.

Whether you choose to set out on your own for a morning ramble, join a guided hiking tour, or shoulder your pack for an ambitious multi-day trek, experiencing the Cotswolds on foot is an absolute must. With miles upon miles of scenic trails right at your doorstep, you'll never be far from the opportunity to immerse yourself in the region's undulating rural landscapes and breath-taking vistas. It's the perfect way to slow down, exercise your body and spirit, and truly discover the heart and soul of the Cotswolds.

- Cycling Routes

With its gently rolling hills, winding country lanes, and vast network of quiet back roads, the Cotswolds is a cyclist's dream destination. Whether you're an avid road cyclist looking to clock some miles or a casual rider hoping to explore at a leisurely pace, the region offers an incredible variety of routes to suit all levels.

For many, the joy of cycling in the Cotswolds is the chance to experience the iconic scenery at handlebar level – winding through tiny villages of honey-colored stone, alongside babbling brooks and ancient woodlands, and across the patchwork landscapes of farm fields and meadows. With little traffic and constantly changing views, it's easy to understand why this area has become a mecca for two-wheeled adventurers.

One of the best ways for visitors to experience Cotswold cycling is to join an organized tour led by local experts and guides. Numerous companies like Go Cyclo-Cotswolds and Cotswold Cycle Tours offer guided day trips and multi-day cycling holidays with custom-created routes.

On a typical day tour, you may set out from a picturesque village like Bourton-on-the-Water for a 25-30 mile loop through the heart of the northern Cotswolds. The ride will take you along quintessentially English lanes, ducking between ancient drystone walls as you pass through hamlets with names like Clapton and Little Rissington. There will be ample opportunities to stop for photos, explore village churches, and refuel at traditional pubs along the way. The expert guides provide full narrative on the history and sights as you ride.

Multi-day tours offer the chance to experience a greater diversity of the Cotswold landscapes. You may spend several days cycling between medieval market towns like Stow-on-the-Wold and Chipping Campden, staying in charming village inns each night. Companies take care of all the logistics like luggage transfers so you can focus solely on pedaling and taking in the scenery.

For those who prefer to go it alone and create their own routes, an extensive network of on and off-road trails awaits. A great option is the Cotswold Line Cycle Route, a 55-mile signed circular trail that starts and ends in Stratford-upon-Avon. Passing through idyllic villages like Chipping Campden, Moreton-in-Marsh, and Stow-on-the-Wold, the trail makes use of former railway paths and quiet back roads to create a scenic ride through archetypal Cotswold countryside.

Cyclists looking for a bigger challenge can test their mettle on the Cotswold Compact Trail, a 90-mile loop taking in the southern reaches of the region. This mostly off-road trail follows an undulating route along bridleways, byways and quiet lanes, passing by stately homes, castles, pristine rivers, and through dense ancient woodlands.

No visit to the Cotswolds would be complete without at least attempting part of the 102-mile Cotswold Way National Trail on two wheels. Although the full trail is optimized more for walking, many sections are suited for mountain bikers or cyclocross bikes. The views from the trail's high points along the Cotswold escarpment are simply breathtaking. Riders can follow the trail for as short or as long a stretch as they desire.

In recent years, the Cotswolds has also gained acclaim as one of the top gravel and bikepacking destinations in the UK. The rural byways, farm tracks, and bridleways that crisscross the region lend themselves perfectly to adventure riding on mixed terrain. The Cotswold Off-Road Gravel Series hosts a number of organized gravel grinder events each year drawing riders from around the country. With the growing popularity of gravel and adventure bikes, exploring the Cotswolds' more rugged and secluded paths has never been more accessible.

No matter whichh routes or trails you choose to ride, one of the joys of cycling in the Cotswolds is the frequent opportunities to stop and explore the area's countless charming villages. Most rides will pass directly through the center of idyllic hamlets lined with stone cottages, country churches, village greens, and traditional pubs. It's always a delight to park your bike, wander through the pedestrian centers, and soak in the timeless atmosphere.

With its scenic and manageable terrain, incredibly dense network of cycling routes, and wealth of quintessential English countryside sights, the Cotswolds offers cycling experiences for all levels and interests. Mellow day rides, epic long-distance challenges, and everything in between can be found here. For those who love riding bikes, a Cotswolds cycling holiday is an absolute must to experience the region's stunning landscapes and timeless villages at the perfect pace.

- Horseback Riding

With its vast expanses of open countryside, rolling hills, and dense network of bridleways and trails, the Cotswolds region provides the perfect setting for exploring on horseback. Equestrians of all levels can find outstanding riding opportunities amid the area's pastoral landscapes of farmland, woodlands, and those iconic honey-colored stone villages.

For many visitors, one of the greatest pleasures of horseback riding in the Cotswolds is the chance to experience the region's beauty from the saddle at a relaxed pace. Clipping along ancient bridleways and country lanes, you'll be immersed in the sights, sounds, and scents of the great outdoors in a way that's simply not possible in a car or even on foot.

Numerous stables, equestrian centers, and riding schools are found throughout the Cotswolds, offering guided trail rides and riding lessons for riders of all experience levels. Operators like Cotswold Riding near Bourton-on-the-Water provide morning, afternoon, or full-day hacks along meticulously planned routes showcasing the best of the local scenery.

On a typical Cotswold trail ride, you may set out in the morning along winding bridleways, passing through timeless villages of stone cottages with greystone roofs. The routes often traverse a patchwork of fields, meadows, and woodlands divided by ancient, lichen-covered drystone walls. There will be ample opportunities to take in the sights at a relaxed walk, trot, or canter as your guide provides commentary about the history and heritage of the landscapes through which you're passing.

For the more experienced riders, itineraries can be specially tailored to offer faster paces and greater challenging terrain. Cotswold Riding offers full and multi-day hacks including opportunities for exhilarating cross-country canters over open fields and hillsides when conditions allow. More advanced trail rides may also take you along more rugged bridleways and across streams as you explore the furthest reaches of the Cotswolds countryside.

One of the highlights is the chance to follow in the footsteps (or hoof prints) of history by riding along sections of ancient routes like the Cotswold Way National Trail. This 102-mile footpath follows along the Cotswold escarpment, offering incredible views along with historical significance as an ancient walking path used for thousands of years. Certain sections are open to horseback riders, providing a unique perspective on the stunning pastoral scenery.

In addition to guided trail rides, the Cotswolds also provides amazing opportunities for riders to set out on their own with rental horses or by bringing their own mounts. A dense network of official bridleways and byways ribbon throughout the region, providing access to its inner reaches. With the proper maps and route planning, equestrians can set out on half-day, full-day, or even multi-day adventures exploring villages, valleys, hills, and woodlands.

One particularly scenic route starts in the quintessential Cotswold village of Bourton-on-the-Water and takes riders through the bucolic hamlets of Lower Slaughter and Upper Slaughter, following along the River Eye. The terrain is gentle, comprised mainly of pastures and fields. Other fantastic self-guided rides can be found branching out from Chipping Campden, Stow-on-the-Wold, Winchcombe, and other centrally located villages. With proper maps and resources from the local stables, riders can craft their own adventures.

For those seeking pure adrenaline and adventure on horseback, the Cotswolds offers outstanding opportunities for trail riding through beautiful private estates. Destinations like the outstanding Batsford Estate near Moreton-in-Marsh provide guided and self-guided rides through their sprawling grounds of parklands, formal gardens, lakes, and woodlands. More daring riders can gallop along bridleways and across open fields with the wind rushing through their hair.

No matter what level of adventure or pace you prefer, the stunning scenery of the Cotswold countryside takes on an entirely new perspective from the back of a horse. The smells of the hedgerows, the warmth of your horse's rhythm, the timeless villages drifting by – it all comes together into an incredible sensory experience that is simply unforgettable. Exploring this region on horseback is to find a connection with the landscapes and heritage that's not possible any other way.

So for any rider or equestrian enthusiast visiting the Cotswolds, horseback riding absolutely must be on the agenda. Whether joining a casual group trail ride or plotting an ambitious self-guided equine adventure, opportunities abound to discover the iconic villages, rolling hills, tranquil waterways, and country lanes of this sublime rural region from a true rider's perspective. It's an outdoor activity that will leave you with memories to cherish forever.

- Hot Air Balloon Rides

For an unforgettable perspective on the picture-perfect Cotswold landscapes, few experiences can match the magic of drifting serenely over the countryside in a hot air balloon. Numerous companies offer balloon flights launching from locations across the region, giving visitors a front-row seat to admire the rolling hills, patchwork fields, and quintessential stone villages from breathtaking heights.

A hot air balloon ride over the Cotswolds begins with an incredibly early start, usually meeting the ground crew around 6 AM as the first rays of dawn start to illuminate the horizon. This early launch time is ideal for catching the calmest winds and most stable air currents for smooth flying conditions. As you arrive at the launch site, which could be anywhere from a park to a farmer's field, the excitement builds as the huge balloon is inflated and prepared for flight.

Once the basket is uprighted and secure, you'll join the group of around 12-16 fellow passengers, helping the crew by holding the mouth of the balloon open as fiery blasts of air are shot in to inflate it. In a matter of minutes, the brightly colored fabric swells into its full teardrop shape towering stories overhead.

With one final blast of heat, the basket leaves the ground and you begin your peaceful ascent, rising up and up until the Cotswolds' bucolic countryside unfurls in a breathtaking panorama below. The world falls away and you enter a profound sense of tranquility as you drift along on gentle winds over a landscape of patchwork fields, winding country lanes, ancient woodlands, tiny hamlets, and manor houses.

Depending on the winds, your pilot will steer the balloon toward areas of particular scenic interest like the archetypal villages of Bourton-on-the-Water, Lower Slaughter, or Stanway. As you lazily float along at heights ranging from just a few hundred feet up to nearly a mile high, you'll be able to appreciate the built and natural environments in a way that is simply not possible from the ground.

One moment, you may be soaring above the rooftops of a medieval market town, admiring the patterns of cottages and church spires nestled along winding streets. The next, you'll have an eagle's perspective on herds of grazing sheep or deer in woodlands and fields carved out of the hillsides by centuries of farming. Then you may find yourself drifting alongside the Cotswold escarpment and escarpment Edge, marveling at the wide vistas and feeling on top of the world.

Throughout the journey, your experienced pilot will use the balloon's altitude to read the air currents, making subtle adjustments to the heat and direction to keep you smoothly floating along. He or she will also serve as your guide to the sights below, pointing out villages, estates, and landmarks while also sharing facts about the heritage and stories of the Cotswolds terrain you're crossing over.

After an hour or so of serene drifting, the pilot will begin looking for a suitable field to land the balloon. As the ground team follows along in their vehicle, they'll help select and prepare the landing site. As the massive balloon rapidly descends back to earth, you'll experience a brief burst of adrenaline before making a gentle touchdown. The ground crew will be there in an instant to secure the basket as you climb out in a field you had only been admiring from above moments earlier.

No hot air balloon experience in the Cotswolds would be complete without joining your pilot and crew to toast your successful flight with a glass of chilled champagne or orange juice. As you sip and celebrate having joined the incredibly small percentage of people who have seen the Cotswolds from a hot air balloon, you can revel in the memories of your unique aerial journey.

Companies like Billowing Bassoons offer a variety of balloon ride options, from traditional dawn flights to Champagne breakfast and evening sunset experiences. For avid photographers, some operators will even design a customized aerial sightseeing tour tailored to giving you the perfect light, viewpoints, and hover times to capture incredible shots of classic Cotswold scenery and villages.

Whether you opt for a serene morning drift or a colorful sunset flight, experiencing the Cotswolds from a hot air balloon provides an utterly magical perspective that will be seared into your memories forever. The sense of tranquility, the spectacular views unlocked, the villages and landscapes revealed in their entirety – it all combines into an adventure that is simply not possible through any other means. For an unforgettable new vantage point on the iconic English countryside, a balloon ride is an absolute must.

- Golf Courses

With its rolling landscapes, pristine countryside setting, and numerous outstanding courses, the Cotswolds has rightfully earned a reputation as one of England's premier golf destinations. Golfers at every level will find incredible options to test their game amid the region's bucolic scenery of gentle hills, valleys, woodlands, and villages built from iconic honey-colored stone.

For many visiting golfers, the chance to tee it up at historic, championship-caliber courses is a major draw. The Cotswolds is home to several of England's most prestigious and highly-ranked layouts that have hosted major professional and amateur events. At the same time, the region boasts a wealth of excellent yet affordable public and resort courses perfect for an enjoyable holiday round.

Any discussion of Cotswolds golf must start with Naunton Downs Golf Club. Established in 1899, this challenging and scenic course is routinely ranked among the top 100 in the world. Its fairways, carved through ancient beechwoods and along the tops of hills, demand skilled play while rewarding golfers with awe-inspiring views across the Cotswold countryside and Windrush Valley. Naunton has played host to the Brabazon Trophy, one of the most prestigious events in British amateur golf.

Another Cotswold layout steeped in history and acclaim is Broadway Golf Club. This parkland-style design, surrounded by the landscapes that inspired artistic giants like John Singer Sargent, dates back to 1895. Its perfectly manicured fairways, greens, and rough areas blend beautifully into the scenery of mature trees, streams, and distant hills. While not quite as formidable as Naunton, Broadway's challenging track has hosted many championship events over the decades.

For a golf experience steeped in tradition and ambiance, pay a visit to Stoke Park. Located on the historic grounds of a former royal estate, Stoke Park offers 27 holes set among idyllic parkland, ornamental gardens, and beautiful water features. Golfers at all levels will appreciate the variety of tee placements that make this venue enjoyable for everyone. The charming historic clubhouse and facilities make Stoke Park the perfect place for a full-day golf getaway.

Those looking for stellar yet affordable public golf should make a tee time at Cirencester Golf Club. Established in 1892, this classic parkland track in the heart of the Cotswolds offers an ideal balance of challenge and playability. Water hazards, elevation changes, and tree-lined fairways make for an engaging round surrounded by incredible scenery. With weekday green fees hovering around £30, Cirencester is the perfect option for budget-conscious and casual holidaymakers.

Thrill-seekers, meanwhile, will want to check out Oakridge Golf Club near Cheltenham. This spectacular modern design, opened in 2003, features a bold layout carved through rolling terrain with dramatic elevation changes on nearly every hole. From soaring tee boxes to tricky greens perched on ledges, Oakridge will rigorously test a player's skills. The striking wooden clubhouse and luxurious practice facilities make it a first-class golf destination.

For those seeking luxury golf and all the amenities of a resort stay, the Cotswolds is home to several outstanding options as well. Golfers at Feldon Valley near Stratford-upon-Avon can enjoy 36 holes of championship play while staying at the wonderful onsite hotel and spa. The resort's courses blend seamlessly into the beautiful natural landscapes of the countryside.

Similarly, Cumberwell Park offers a tranquil yet challenging round of golf along with spa treatments, indoor and outdoor pools, and deluxe accommodations in a historic manor house setting. Golf groups and those looking for a serene golf getaway will find Cumberwell Park to be the perfect fit.

Beyond just the layouts themselves, one of the great joys of golfing in the Cotswolds is the environment and scenery itself. Nearly every course takes advantage of the region's iconic rural terrain – from sweeping hillside vistas to placid streams, flower-lined fairways to ancient stone walls and villages in the distance. The setting truly is second-to-none.

Numerous local touring companies offer stay-and-play golf packages giving visitors the chance to combine tee times at different venues along with accommodation at charming village inns, manors, or B&Bs. It's an ideal way to fully immerse yourself in the Cotswolds golf experience over a multi-day trip while having all the details taken care of.

With such a wide array of championship designs, budget-friendly community tracks, cutting-edge resort courses, and outstanding natural surroundings, it's easy to understand why the Cotswolds has become a mecca for golfers. Whether you're a passionate player looking to check iconic layouts off your bucket list or simply a casual enthusiast hoping to play a relaxed round amid sublime scenery, the Cotswold golf scene truly has something for everyone. Teeing it up while surrounded by the region's gentle hills, stone villages, and tranquility guarantees an unforgettable golf experience.

- Fishing Spots

With its myriad rivers, streams, lakes, and ponds flowing through the gently rolling Cotswold countryside, the region offers a truly outstanding array of fishing opportunities for anglers of all skill levels. From tranquil river beats thick with trout to historic manmade lakes and reservoirs stocked with an array of species, there are seemingly endless possibilities for enjoying a day's fishing amid the iconic rural landscapes.

For many, the quintessential Cotswolds fishing experience revolves around the area's numerous chalk streams and rivers. Springs and aquifers filter up through the underlying limestone to create waterways with a unique chemical makeup and environment perfect for nurturing wild brown trout, grayling, and other species. The most renowned streams include the Windrush, Coln, Leach, and Eye, among others.

Day tickets can be purchased to fish certain stretches of these rivers in season, granting access to some truly beautiful and serene environments. Imagine wading into the knee-deep, crystal clear waters of the River Coln, flanked by grassy banks, weeping willows, and timeless Cotswold stone villages in the background. As your fly drifts downstream, you'll scan the currents and pools for signs of a rise as you pursue the elusive and wily wild brown trout that make their home here.

Chalkstreams like the Coln, Leach, and Windrush have been luring anglers and fly fishermen for generations thanks to the combination of their sublime scenery, challenging fishing conditions, and highly productive waters. Guided fishing tours provide a fantastic introduction, teaching the specialized techniques and local knowledge to help you land that prized trout. Services like Cotswold Fly Fishing offer full and half-day outings with expert guides.

While river fishing makes up a large part of the angling scene, the Cotswolds is also home to some truly stunning stillwater fisheries as well. A number of historic reservoirs, estate lakes, and purpose-built modern facilities offer unsurpassed fishing for carp, trout, tench, bream, and many other species in incredible scenic settings.

One of the most well-known and iconic venues is the Cotswold Water Park, comprised of over 150 lakes and waterways just south of Cirencester. Fed by natural springs and aquifers, these expansive lakes were formed from old quarry workings over the past few centuries. Today, the Cotswold Water Park has become one of the largest and most diverse inland fisheries in the country, with different lakes managed as everything from prime trout waters to specimen carp havens. The scenery is strikingly beautiful, with mature trees, grassy banks, and swans dotting the shorelines.

For those seeking secluded lakeside serenity, Lodge Park near Sherbourne offers excellent fishing amid its historic estate grounds. The main lake dates back to the 1700s and is stocked with tench, bream, and other coarse species, while additional pools and ponds provide further opportunities to cast a line. Day tickets give you full access to explore and find that perfect spot to relax among the manicured gardens and countryside landscapes.

Another option beloved by anglers is the Mayfield Lakes, an exclusive private membership venue between Cheltenham and Gloucester. With over 50 acres of lakes and surrounding woodlands, Mayfield has been impeccably developed for serious game anglers targeting carp, tench, bream, and other coarse species. Mature trees line the banks, affording plenty of coverage and shady spots to settle in. The well-maintained facilities make Mayfield feel like a true private retreat, the perfect place to spend a day in blissful angling tranquility.

The options continue with prime trout lakes at the Cotswold Hills Fishery, open carp and coarse fishing at Bossard Lakes, and the pristine fly fishing at Greenlake itself. No matter your skill level or target species, there are seemingly endless stillwater venues to explore throughout the Cotswold countryside.

Countless rivers, streams, and lakes flow through landscapes of iconic pastoral beauty – that simple fact alone makes the Cotswolds one of the most amazing angling destinations in all of England. But when combined with the region's heritage as a fishing mecca stretching back centuries and the incredible variety of top-tier stillwater fisheries, it becomes clear why anglers continually flock here.

Whether you're an expert fly fisher stalking wild trout on a chalk stream, a casual angler looking to wile away a day along the banks of a reservoir, or an avid specialist pursuing massive carp from lakes set in classic English gardens and grounds, the Cotswolds delivers an experience to remember. With so many acclaimed fishing spots to discover, any angler visiting the region is spoiled for choice on where to cast their line and soak in the unparalleled scenery.

Chapter 5

Exploring Cotswold's' History and Culture

- Cotswold Museums

With roots stretching back thousands of years, the Cotswolds is an area steeped in incredibly rich history and heritage. For visitors hoping to dive deeper into the stories, traditions, and figures that have shaped this iconic English countryside, the region is home to an outstanding array of fascinating museums. From grand country estates to charming village collections, these museums offer the perfect opportunity to uncover the Cotswolds' captivating narratives.

One of the must-visit museums is Blenheim Palace near Woodstock. This monumental 18th century residence was the birthplace of Sir Winston Churchill and a masterpiece of English Baroque architecture. A tour through Blenheim's opulent state rooms, galleries, and grounds provides incredible insight into the history of English nobility, politics, and design. Highlights include the stunning Great Hall, Churchill's birth room, the Palace's priceless collection of tapestries and portraits, and the Capability Brown-designed landscaped gardens. Blenheim allows visitors to experience firsthand the splendor and grandeur of an English country estate at its finest.

In the heart of Chipping Campden village, the Courtroom and Police Museum immerses visitors in the rich judicial heritage of the Cotswolds dating back to the 17th century. This wonderfully preserved historic courtroom was where local magistrates passed judgement on all manner of civil and criminal cases. The museum's recreated police room, jail cells, and exhibits showcase law and order from the 1600s-1800s. Docents provide fantastic guided tours brining the stories of colorful local criminals and historic trials to life.

To truly appreciate the Cotswolds region's history as the center of England's medieval wool trade, a visit to the CotswoldsWoollenUppliers Museum in Cheltenham is an absolute must. This standout museum is housed in a beautifully restored Regency era mill building and is fully dedicated to preserving the tools, machinery, and legacy of the local wool industry. Through interactive exhibits, galleries of artifacts, and live spinning and weaving demonstrations, visitors gain insight into the full wool manufacturing process from fleece to finished fabric. The restored equipment, recreated mill worker housing, and informative displays make this an unforgettable glimpse into the backbone of the Cotswolds' historic economy.

Providing a window into rural English life from centuries ago is the Gloucestershire Folk Museum, set in the historic market town of Bourton-on-the-Water. Spread across two sites, the museum features a wealth of historic buildings that have been carefully gathered and relocated from villages across the county. Highlights include a 15th century merchant's house, tinsmith's workshop, and a Victorian Catholic chapel, fully preserved and furnished to their original states. It's a wonderland for history lovers, offering the unique experience of walking through authentically recreated spaces that would have been found in a typical Gloucestershire village hundreds of years in the past.

Within the regal grounds of Woodchester Park, the Woodchester Valley Village Museum shares the compelling stories of the estate's former workforce and tenants. Exhibits, furnished cottages, and even an entire recreated village street illuminate the challenging living and working conditions of the workers who toiled in the estate's fields, homes, and industry. Audio tours vividly narrate the residents' day-to-day lives and provide insight into the stark contrasts between the wealthy landowners and the common laborers who facilitated their lavish lifestyles.

Beyond the permanent displays, many of the Cotswolds' manors, churches, and heritage sites host rotating special exhibitions covering themes like archeology, local military history, costume/fashion, and fine arts. These offer even more in-depth and often overlooked perspectives on the region's past.

What makes exploring the Cotswolds' museums so rewarding is the ability to gain insights directly from the places and spaces where history actually unfolded. From the aristocratic luxury of a country manor to the humble living quarters of estate workers, from preserved places of worship to historic mills and industries, these museums provide a tangible connection to the stories and narratives of those who occupied these landscapes in centuries past.

Visiting exhibitions, carefully preserved artifacts, perfectly recreated environments, and compelling interactive displays make the region's rich heritage spring vibrantly to life for the modern visitor. The Cotswolds' many outstanding museums offer the chance to immerse yourself in history simply not possible through reading alone. They are windows into the localized narratives that make this area so unique and endlessly fascinating. Any journey through the Cotswolds would be incomplete without taking the time to experience its culture and legacy through the museums and heritage sites that carefully safeguard its remarkable past.

- Historic Churches

The gentle hills, valleys, and villages of the Cotswolds are adorned with an astonishing number of historic churches and cathedrals that have stood as focal points of local communities for centuries. These hallowed spaces of worship offer more than just architectural marvels – they provide profound connections to the region's rich spiritual heritage and the people who built and cherished them over generations.

From the soaring gothic splendor of great cathedrals to humble village churches crafted of iconic Cotswold stone, these ecclesiastical buildings open windows into the history and culture of the communities they have served. Whether admiring detailed craftsmanship, uncovering the tales of legendary figures who passed through their doors, or simply contemplating in the stillness of their ancient shadows, exploring the Cotswolds' churches is an experience filled with deeper meaning.

The undisputed crown jewel is Gloucester Cathedral, an awe-inspiring edifice that has dominated the city's skyline for over 900 years. This massive cathedral exemplifies the finest gothic architecture, from its deeply sculpted stone façade to the extraordinary stained glass windows, ribbed vaulting, and fan-vaulted cloisters. Highlights include the spectacular east window depicting the binding of the Bible and the tomb of Edward II. But beyond its architectural majesty, the cathedral's greatest significance lies in its role as the spiritual heart of the Cotswolds. Generations of local faithful have gathered in its hallowed halls for worship, celebration, and solace over nearly a millennium.

Nearby in Tewkesbury, the spectacular Norman-era abbey church is another ecclesiastical monument not to be missed. With roots dating back over 900 years, the abbey is renowned for its massive crossing tower soaring over 150 feet, richly decorated choir, and awe-inspiring vaulted nave. The abbey's turbulent history has seen it besieged and partially destroyed in conflicts over the centuries. But it stands today as an enduring symbol of the faith that has guided local communities through both triumphs and struggles.

While the great cathedrals and abbeys amaze with their grandeur, the smaller village churches scattered throughout the Cotswolds countryside offer their own unique charm and deep heritage. Visitors will find beautifully preserved examples in nearly every town, some so ancient their foundations date back over 1,000 years to the Saxon era.

St. Andrew's Church in Sevenhampton provides a wonderful example of a traditional Cotswold parish church. Parts of the stone exterior walls and tower extend back to the 11th century while later additions were completed in the 15th century gothic style. Inside the unassuming exterior, you'll find a breathtaking Norman-era nave with trigonal stone columns and intricately carved capitals. Viewing the simple beauty through the eyes of those who have worshipped here for centuries is a powerful experience.

The Church of St. John the Baptist in Cirencester features Saxon elements dating back over 1,000 years amidst later medieval additions. Here you can view a rare example of a complete Saxon door frame, plus Anglo-Saxon crosses and relics unearthed on the site. Every aspect offers clues into the daily lives of the earliest Christianized villages in the region.

Regardless of one's personal faith or spiritual beliefs, exploring the Cotswolds' historic churches provides a singularly evocative experience. Beyond their architectural splendor, these hallowed spaces offer an intimate connection to the generations of faithful whose devotion quite literally constructed and sustained them over centuries. As you wander their naves, gaze upon their monuments, and admire their craftsmanship, you gain profound insights into the hopes, struggles, and traditions that have defined communities here since the earliest days of Christianity's arrival.

Many churches also hold ties to legendary figures whose stories have become interwoven with local lore. The Church of St. Mary in Fairford is home to outstanding medieval stained glass depicting scenes from the Bible that are among the finest in England. They were paid for by the wealthy merchant John Tame in an act of penance to reconcile acts of fraud and deception in his business practices. In Northleach, you can view the Church of St. Peter & St. Paul associated with the so-called "Cotswold Olympic" founder Robert Dover, an attorney who initiated local sporting events each year after services on Whitsunday. Stories like these bring the church's ancient stones to life.

When wandering through the Cotswolds region, these historic churches will beckon you at nearly every turn, both with their breathtaking architecture and their profound connections to the region's cultural narrative. Opportunities to attend services, appreciate the craftsmanship and artistry of their accoutrements, and uncover the stories hidden within their very walls await all who step through their doors with curiosity and openness. For those with any interest in history, spirituality, art, or connecting with the Cotswolds' boundless heritage, exploring these time-honored houses of worship is an absolute must.

- Cotswold Woollen Weavers

The story of the Cotswolds is inextricably linked to the rise and fall of the region's woollen weaving industry. For centuries, the spinning, dyeing, weaving, and finishing of wool was the driving economic force that created immense wealth, influenced architecture, and defined the very character of Cotswold communities. Understanding the legacy of these skilled woollen weavers provides profound insights into the Cotswolds' cultural identity.

The origins of the Cotswolds wool trade can be traced back over a thousand years to the fertile pastures and flocks of sheep that grazed the area's limestone hills and valleys. This environment produced an incredibly high-quality wool ideal for producing warmth-retaining cloth. Medieval merchants and traders were quick to recognize wool's value, encouraging local villagers to take up the labor-intensive work of spinning and weaving.

By the 13th and 14th centuries, the demand for Cotswold wool cloth was immense, both within England and across Europe. Small villages like Campden, Northleach, and Chipping Norton emerged as weaving capitals. Entire communities became devoted to the intricate process, with individual households specializing in the various steps from scouring to carding, spinning to dyeing, weaving to finishing and fulling.

The Cotswold farmers-turned-weavers took great pride in their skills. They developed their own unique woollen cloth characterized by its thick, dense nap and warmth-retaining properties. Highly sought after, this "Cotswold cloth" was exported as far away as Florence and Venice, making regional traders incredibly wealthy.

The tremendous profits generated allowed the Cotswold wool barons to invest in monumental churches and manor houses, many of which can still be admired today for their architectural majesty and Cotswold stone craftsmanship. Entire towns took on distinctive layouts centered around the industry, including the long, straight "grobust" roads built to facilitate the drying of cloth after the fulling process was completed.

Visitors to the region can still see remnants of the widespread wool trade in the towns and buildings themselves. In the 17th century market town of Marshfield, historic buildings like the "Puck House" along Pigs Quoiting Street were the former homes of prosperous clothiers with enormous attic spaces devoted to their spinning and carding operations. Along Rack Lane, long rows of exterior racks can still be seen where dyed wool was hung to dry.

In Chipping Campden, the iconic Wool Market Hall still features circular wool sack holders carved into its stone exterior where merchants would display their highest quality wools for sale. Campden's entire historic center is dotted with grand towered mansions once occupied by wealthy clothiers at the height of the wool trade.

As wealth accrued, the local weavers began to branch out into banking and the legal professions. Many graduates of the wool trade went on to become influential merchants and politicians. But by the late 18th century, competition from Yorkshire mills coupled with a struggling export trade brought the Cotswolds' wool supremacy to an end. One by one, weavers ceased production and villages contracted.

Today, the CotswoldsWoollen Weavers museum in Cheltenham provides an immersive living history experience delving into every facet of the region's most pivotal industry. Hosted inside a restored Regency wool mill, exhibitions utilize reconstructed machines and guides demonstrating manual wool working processes to tell the full story. Visitors can see original tools, looms, and devices used in washing, carding, dyeing, spinning and finishing cloth.

As you wander through the exhibits, you gain a true understanding of the incredible skill, craftsmanship, and labor that went into producing the wool cloth the Cotswolds was once renowned for across Europe. It was not just a commercial enterprise, but an art form born of centuries of tradition and innovation.

- Cotswold Arts and Crafts

The Cotswolds' incredibly rich artistic heritage stretches back centuries, making it one of England's most important centers for traditional arts, crafts, and creative expression. From stonemasons who constructed the region's iconic cottages and churches to hand-loom weavers, potters, furniture makers, and more, generations of skilled artisans have left an indelible mark on the Cotswolds' character and aesthetic.

For modern visitors, engaging with the Cotswolds' vibrant arts and crafts scene is the perfect way to gain insights into local history while connecting with contemporary craftspeople carrying traditions into the 21st century. The region today remains a thriving hub of creative energy where both ancient and modern crafts can be observed, studied, and collected.

At the heart of the Cotswold craft heritage is the region's distinctive building material – the golden-colored Cotswold oolitic limestone. This sedimentary stone has been quarried here for centuries to construct everything from humble cottages and barns to grand manor houses and churches. Developed over generations, Cotswold masonry and stonecraft represent a profound artisanal skill passed from master to apprentice over centuries.

Visitors can see these skilled stone workers practicing their craft at places like the Stonemasons at Work museum in Winchcombe. Here, a team of masons work daily shaping raw Cotswold stone into lintels, masonry, sculptures, and architectural elements. They use traditional mallet and chisel methods handed down through generations to carve intricate shapes and adornments. The exhibitions showcase examples of their craftsmanship while informative videos and guides explain the historic significance and methods of Cotswold stonemasonry.

This stone craftsmanship is also on display in the countless Cotswold cottages, barns, churches, and manors that give the region its iconic look. The stonemasons' artistry is evidenced in intricately carved door and window surrounds, gateways, sills, fireplaces, gabled rooflines, and more details throughout the built environment. Guided walking tours through towns like Winchcombe provide insights into how to identify different stone styles, designs, and motifs on historic buildings.

No discussion of Cotswold cultural heritage would be complete without examining the region's long wool weaving and textile tradition. From the medieval wool boom to the 19th century Arts and Crafts movement revival, woven materials have been an essential Cotswold creative expression for over a thousand years.

Today, visitors can view working demonstrations and purchase textiles from craftspeople continuing that legacy. The idyllic village of Marshfield is home to a community of hand loom weavers, with the Marshfield Weaver's workshop showcasing historic floor looms in action. The Cotswold Craftsmen shop features handwoven blankets, throws, and garments created using traditional methods and natural dye processes. Nearby towns like Northleach also host annual wool craft events and exhibitions.

Pottery is another quintessential Cotswold craft form that has flourished for centuries. Guided by the abundance of regional clay sources, generations of skilled potters produced glazed slipware, utilitarian wares, and ceramic art that both beautified local homes and found consumers across England.

In Woodstock, the Cotswold Pottery immerses visitors in this rich clay tradition. Located in a restored 17th century kiln house, the museum showcases historic regional ceramics while modern artisans create and fire decorative and functional pieces nearby. Similarly in Winchcombe, visitors can view skilled potters at work on kick wheels at the Gloucestershire Pottery Centre. They'll learn time-honored techniques and styles like bat stamping that make Cotswold ceramics so distinctive.

Arts and crafts from wood are also deeply rooted in Cotswold culture, especially furniture making, carvings, and woodturning. From historic cabinet makers and chair bodgers to artisans restoring architectural elements and creating fine art sculptures, wood crafts have always been integral to both form and function here.

Today, carvers, turners, sculptors, and furniture makers abound, many working with traditional tools and techniques passed down over generations. Shops like Halls the Furniture Makers in Chipping Campden and Made in Isbourne in Lower Slaughter showcase handcrafted wares. The galleries at Stratford-upon-Avon's Henley Street allow browsing an incredible array of contemporary turned wood creations from acclaimed craftspeople working in the rich Cotswold tradition.

In addition to exploring studios, galleries, and demonstrations, visitors can discover the Cotswolds' artistic legacy through outlets like the Gloucestershire Guild of Craftsmen. This organization, founded in the 1930s, brings together dozens of master artisans working in media from metal to textiles. The Guild hosts craft fairs and open studio trails enabling visitors to explore workshops, meet makers, and purchase one-of-a-kind artworks and goods.

By viewing and supporting the region's modern makers, collectors forge connections to the history, stories, and techniques that have shaped Cotswold arts and crafts for centuries. They engage with the continuation of production methods, aesthetics, and material usage that have defined the creative spirit of the region across generations. Exploring local studios, workshops, museums, and galleries opens doorways to understanding the living traditions that make the Cotswolds such an enduring and authentic creative hub.

Chapter 6

Local Cuisine and Dining

- Local Pubs and Restaurants

1. Gloucestershire Old Spot Pork

OPEN HOURS

Sun - Sat

11:00 AM - 8:30 PM

DESCRIPTION: Glorious Gloucestershire Old Spot pork, locally raised in the Cotswolds, is visually striking with its cherry-red lean muscle laced with ribbons of snowy white fat. This fat marbling gives the meat a uniquely succulent flavor and tender texture. Slow roasting an Old Spot pork belly yields mouthwatering meat coated in crackling so crunchy it shatters. Traditional recipes like pork pies and sausages brilliantly showcase the breed's rich taste. When dining at a Cotswolds pub, be sure to order dishes that highlight Old Spot pork, such as fork-tender pork shoulder braised for hours or baked ham hock served alongside refreshing, tangy applesauce. The distinctive marbling and mellow flavor of the locally reared Old Spots make it a cherished ingredient for quintessential Cotswold fare. Savoring these heritage breed pigs is an unmissable part of the food culture in this picturesque region of England.

MEALS:

- Lunch
- Dinner
- Brunch

FEATURES:

- Outdoor Seating
- Seating
- Parking Available
- Free off-street parking
- Highchairs Available
- Serves Alcohol
- Full Bar
- Accepts Mastercard
- Accepts Visa
- Free Wifi
- Reservations

- Wheelchair Accessible
- Accepts Credit Cards
- Table Service
- Gift Cards Available

PRICE RANGE: $9 - $30

CUISINES:

- British
- Pub
- Dining bars

SPECIALTY:

- Vegetarian Friendly
- Vegan Options
- Gluten Free Options

ADDRESS: Gloucester Old Spot Tewkesbury Road Elmstone Hardwick, Tewkesbury Road, Cheltenham GL51 9SY England

TELEPHONE: +44 1242 680321

EMAIL: eat@thegloucesteroldspot.co.uk

WEBSITE: https://www.thegloucesteroldspot.co.uk/

2. *The Old Bakery Tearoom*

OPEN HOURS

Mon – Sat 10:30 AM - 4:00 PM,

Closed on Thursdays

DESCRIPTION: For 19 years, Jackie and Alan have proudly operated The Old Bakery Tearoom, upholding exceptional service and quality. Nearly everything gracing the menu is made in-house using wholesome ingredients, from soups and dressings to jams and baked goods. Scones and cakes emerge piping-hot and fresh from the ovens daily. Ethically-sourced local coffee and tea fill cups and teapots. In addition to classic tea fare, gluten-free and vegetarian options abound, including homemade gluten-free scones perfect for cream teas.

The Tearoom exudes warmth and hominess, drawing loyal regulars and new visitors alike. Clean canine companions are also welcome! Stop in Tuesdays through Saturdays 10:30am-4pm for homestyle baking, aromatic coffee and tea, and a quintessential Cotswolds tearoom experience mastered by Jackie and Alan over nearly two decades. Savor time-honored flavors and sincere hospitality at this cherished local gem.

MEALS:

- Lunch
- Brunch
- Breakfast
- Drinks

FEATURES:

- Seating
- Highchairs Available
- Wheelchair Accessible
- Accepts Mastercard
- Accepts Visa
- Reservations
- Accepts Credit Cards
- Table Service
- Street Parking
- Accepts American Express
- Dog Friendly

PRICE RANGE: $5 - $19

CUISINES:

- British
- Healthy

SPECIALTY:

- Vegetarian Friendly
- Gluten Free Options
- Vegan Options

ADDRESS: Digbeth Street 4 Fountain Court, Stow-on-the-Wold GL54 1BN England

TELEPHONE: +44 1451 832172

EMAIL: alanslough@btinternet.com

WEBSITE: https://www.theoldbakerytearoom.co.uk/

3. *Restaurant Journey*

OPEN HOURS

Wed – Sat 7:00 PM - 11:00 PM
Closed on Monday, Tuesday and
Sunday.

DESCRIPTION: Restaurant Journey takes diners on a global culinary adventure with its inventive tasting menus infused with flavors from around the world. Daring food combinations like Singapore chili crab followed by sticky toffee pudding bring unique fusion flair. The kitchen playfully reimagines cuisines both familiar and exotic, while emphasizing fresh local ingredients.

The moody lighting and lively music create an immersive, high-energy atmosphere. Journey captures the spirit of exploration through audaciously crafted dishes, experimental cocktail pairings, and an unconventional fine dining experience. From savoring street food inspirations to embarking on the 12-course tasting voyage, the menu thrills palates with its bold twists on tradition. At Restaurant Journey, expectations are delightedly subverted. Embark on a voyage for the senses, where adventurous eaters are rewarded with global tastes crafted through the lens of innovation and fun.

MEALS:

- Dinner

FEATURES:

- Reservations
- Seating
- Serves Alcohol
- Full Bar
- Accepts Credit Cards
- Table Service
- Gift Cards Available

PRICE RANGE: $101 - $139

CUISINES:

- Contemporary
- International

- Fusion

SPECIALTY:

- Vegetarian
  Friendly

ADDRESS: 12 Bath Road, Cheltenham GL53 7HA England

TELEPHONE: +44 1242 805158

EMAIL: info@restaurantjourney.co.uk

WEBSITE: https://restaurantjourney.co.uk/

4. *Karibu - Vegan Bar & Kitchen*

OPEN HOURS

- Tue – Thur 5:30 PM
  - 9:00 PM
- Fri

12:30 PM - 3:00 PM

5:30 PM - 10:00 PM

- Sat

12:30 PM - 3:00 PM

5:30 PM - 10:00 PM

- Closed on Mondays and Sundays

DESCRIPTION: Karibu, dreamed up by the former chef behind Indie Veggie, pioneers as Stroud's first and only vegan bar and eatery. The menu celebrates plant-based cuisine from around the globe, like Indian samosas, Mexican nachos and tacos, and hearty burgers with polenta chips. Flexitarians can indulge in family-style sharing plates for a taste of everything. Karibu sources ingredients sustainably and eco-consciously, aligning with its green ethos. The vibe buzzes with community spirit, welcoming all to savor feel-good food and drink. From satisfying three-course dinners to casual plates enjoyed over drinks at the bar, Karibu brings worldly vegan fare home to Stroud. Here, flavorful dishes inventively prove plant-powered cuisine can be comforting yet daring. Karibu's devoted following agrees: the future is vegan, and it's delicious. Pull up a seat in this vibrant, veggie-loving hub.

MEALS:

- Lunch
- Dinner
- Brunch
- Late Night
- Drinks

FEATURES:

- Takeout
- Reservations
- Outdoor Seating
- Seating

- Serves Alcohol
- Full Bar
- Accepts Credit Cards
- Table Service
- Free off-street parking
- Wine and Beer
- Digital Payments
- Cash Only
- Free Wifi
- Family style
- Non-smoking restaurants
- Gift Cards Available

PRICE RANGE: $5 - $16

CUISINES:

- Mexican
- African
- International
- Street Food
- Healthy

SPECIALTY:

- Vegetarian Friendly
- Vegan Options
- Gluten Free Options

ADDRESS: 23 Nelson Street, Stroud GL5 2HH England

TELEPHONE: +44 1453 790695

EMAIL: karibu@eventsology.co.uk

WEBSITE: https://www.karibu23.co.uk/food

5. *The Mahal*

OPEN HOURS

- **Mon – Tue 5:30 PM - 10:00 PM**

- **Wed - Sat**
  12:00 PM - 2:30 PM
  5:30 PM - 10:00 PM
- **Closed on Sundays**

DESCRIPTION: The aptly named Mahal, meaning "palace" in Hindi, transports diners to regal luxury with its sumptuous setting. From the opulent decor to the royal treatment, Mahal envelops guests in splendor. The glittering interior evokes the grandeur of India's grand architectural marvels, an exquisite backdrop for savoring Mahal's artful cuisine. Culinary treasures await behind these palace doors, from complex curries redolent of spice to tender tandoori specialties kissed by fire.

Mahal's attentive service ensures each visit feels like dining with maharajas. Every element converges to create an unforgettable feast for the senses. Within Mahal's jewel-toned walls, discover just how glorious Indian dining can be. From first bite to final farewell, Mahal lives up to its majestic moniker, delivering a dazzling Indian dining experience fit for royalty in the heart of Cheltenham.

MEALS:

- Lunch
- Dinner

FEATURES:

- Reservations
- Seating
- Serves Alcohol
- Full Bar
- Table Service
- Gift Cards Available

PRICE RANGE: $25 - $63

CUISINES:

- Indian
- Asian

SPECIALTY:

- Vegetarian Friendly
- Vegan Options

- Gluten Free Options

ADDRESS: Montpellier Drive, Cheltenham GL50 1TY England

TELEPHONE: +44 1242 226300

EMAIL: dine@themahalrestaurant.com

WEBSITE: https://www.themahalrestaurant.com/

6. *Cotswold Baguettes*

OPEN HOURS

- **Mon - Sat**
  09:00 AM - 3:00 PM
- **Closed on Sundays**

DESCRIPTION: Cotswold Baguettes brings a taste of France to the village high street. The aroma of freshly baked bread wafts from the ovens as baguettes emerge with crackly golden crusts encasing fluffy, cloud-like interiors. Traditional French viennoiseries like croissants and pain au chocolat are prepared daily, beckoning passersby. Rustic, farmhouse-style loaves are crafted from local Cotswolds flour. Sandwiches showcase regional meats and cheeses between slices of just-baked baguette. Beyond bread, Cotswold Baguettes conjures Parisian essence with French macarons, eclairs, tartes and more. The quaint café brews aromatic French press coffee to enjoy alongside baked goods. Whether gathering ingredients for a picnic, seeking a mid-day snack, or picking up the perfect loaf, Cotswold Baguettes brings joy through authentic artisan baking. Stop in and experience the warm hospitality and mouthwatering aromas that have made this beloved village bakery a Cotswolds treasure for years.

MEALS:

- Breakfast
- Brunch
- Lunch

FEATURES:

- Takeout
- Accepts Credit Cards
- Wheelchair Accessible

PRICE RANGE: $25 - $63

CUISINES:

- Fast Food
- Healthy
- British

SPECIALTY:

- Vegetarian Friendly
- Vegan Options
- Gluten Free Options

ADDRESS: Cotswold House Church Street, Stow-on-the-Wold GL54 1BB England

TELEPHONE: +44 1451 831362

EMAIL: enquiries@cotswoldbaguettes.co.uk

WEBSITE: https://www.cotswoldbaguettes.co.uk/

7. *Amalfi*

OPEN HOURS

- **Sun**

12:00 PM - 11:00 PM

- **Mon - Thur**

5:00 PM - 10:00 PM

- **Fri**

12:00 PM - 11:00 PM

DESCRIPTION: Amalfi brings true Italian hospitality and home-cooking to town at this authentic family-run ristorante. The extensive menu brims with beloved dishes from across Italy's diverse culinary landscape, from hearty lasagna al forno to seafood linguine awash in white wine sauce. Recipes perfected through generations feature fresh pasta crafted daily and sauces simmering low and slow. Amalfi prides itself on sourcing premium Italian ingredients to craft each dish with meticulous care. The lively ambience fills with the aroma of tomatoes, garlic and fresh basil. Between bites of wood-fired pizza or spinach ravioli, guests become family at Amalfi's welcoming tables. The genuine warmth and generosity of the owners and staff create a dining experience steeped in old-world charm. For a taste of Italy without leaving home, visit Amalfi to enjoy their passion for sharing cherished regional flavors in a setting of true Italian comfort.

MEALS:

- Dinner
- Lunch
- Brunch

FEATURES:

- Takeout
- Reservations
- Outdoor Seating
- Seating
- Highchairs Available
- Wheelchair Accessible

- Serves Alcohol
- Full Bar
- Free Wifi
- Accepts Credit Cards
- Table Service
- Street Parking
- Free off-street parking
- Wine and Beer
- Digital Payments
- Live Music
- Dog Friendly
- Family style
- Non-smoking restaurants
- Gift Cards Available

PRICE RANGE: $32 - $44

CUISINES:

- Italian
- Pizza
- Mediterranean
- European
- Healthy
- Neapolitan
- Southern-Italian
- Campania
- Tuscan
- Romana
- Lazio
- Sicilian
- Central-Italian

SPECIALTY:

- Vegetarian Friendly
- Vegan Options

- Gluten Free
  Options

ADDRESS: 16 The Old Crown, Market Street, Nailsworth, Stroud GL6 0BX England

TELEPHONE: +44 1453 350432

EMAIL: nailsworthamalfi@gmail.com

WEBSITE: https://amalfi-italian.co.uk/

8. *MUSE Brasserie - Cheltenham*

OPEN HOURS

- **Mon**

5:30 PM - 10:00 PM

- **Tue - Sat**

12:00 PM - 2:00 PM

5:30 PM - 10:00 PM

Closed on Sundays

DESCRIPTION: Muse Brasserie journeys through Europe's cuisines with Chef Franck's flair for fusing flavors. While founded on classic French technique, the menu exudes Franck's adventurous spirit and globetrotting palate. Dishes burst with vibrant spice from India, aromatic stir-fries inspired by Asia, and comfort foods from across the continent. Though daringly diverse, Muse maintains balance through expert skill and artful combinations. The daily offerings present both reinvented brasserie favorites and Franck's signature specialties. The dining room echoes this spirit of cultured exploration in its chic yet relaxed ambience. At Muse, open-minded diners are transported on a voyage across Europe's diverse culinary landscape. With each dish, Franck invites guests to discover new dimensions of flavor as he weaves his international inspirations into cuisine both familiar and exotic. Muse awakens the senses by blending tradition with ingenuity from the far corners of the continent.

MEALS:

- Dinner
- Lunch
- Drinks

FEATURES:

- Gift Cards Available
- Reservations
- Seating
- Highchairs Available
- Serves Alcohol
- Full Bar
- Free Wifi
- Accepts Credit Cards
- Table Service
- Digital Payments

PRICE RANGE: $32 - $44

CUISINES:

- French
- European
- Fusion

SPECIALTY:

- Vegetarian Friendly
- Vegan Options
- Gluten Free Options

ADDRESS: Formal House 60 St. Georges Place, Cheltenham GL50 3PN England

TELEPHONE: +44 1242 239447

EMAIL: dine@musebrasserie.com

WEBSITE: https://www.musebrasserie.com/

- Farmers' Markets

Farmers' markets are a fabulous way to experience the bounty of the Cotswolds countryside while supporting local producers. Here's a guide to some of the best farmers' markets in the region:

Stroud Farmers' Market

Held every Saturday, this award-winning market has over 90 stalls showcasing the best in local food and handmade crafts. Explore stalls piled high with just-picked vegetables, ripe Cotswolds fruit, artisan breads and cheeses. Look for stallholders like Brinkworth Dairy, Lovemore Farm organic meat, and enthusiastic growers who can recommend great recipe ideas. The lively atmosphere with music and street food makes the market a highlight of any visit to Stroud.

Cirencester Farmers' Market

Taking place the 2nd and 4th Saturdays of each month, Cirencester's market features over 50 producers. The stalls are located around the historic Market Place, perfect for grabbing picnic provisions before exploring Cirencester. Seek out goose eggs, seasonal game like pheasant and venison, locally crafted ales, and award-winning charcuterie from the Cotswolds Charcuterie Company based in Tetbury.

Burford Farmers' Market

Discover Burford's scenic High Street lined with stalls of food, garden and craft producers every 2nd and 4th Saturday. Highlights include Suffolk lamb and Hereford beef reared in the Cotswolds, smoked fish and ostrich burgers. Enjoy street food or have a coffee at one of Burford's cafés while listening to live musicians perform.

Bourton-on-the-Water Farmers' Market

One of the liveliest farmer's markets in the Cotswolds takes place every 4th Sunday along Bourton's High Street and village green. Meander past photography, ceramics, jewelry and textiles from local artisans. Treat yourself to take-home food purchases like artisan bread, Cotswold cheeses, homemade pies and delectable cakes. A great place to pick up unique souvenirs too.

Chipping Norton Farmers' Market

Discover the charming market town of Chipping Norton on the 3rd Saturday of the month when its market opens. Over 40 stalls offer Gloucester Old Spot sausages, smoked trout, wooden toys, soaps and candles that make for wonderful gifts. Stop at one of the cafes on the square for tasty brunch made with the farmers' market goodies.

Witney Farmers' Market

Held on the 3rd Friday each month, the Witney market boasts over 50 stalls stretching through the old town center. Sample a dazzling array of local produce, meats, cheeses, cakes and artisan products that display the best of the region's agriculture. Don't miss the piping hot street food like crepes and baked potatoes too.

Farmers' Market Tips

- Ask questions about produce and farming methods to the friendly sellers.
- Bring a large basket or bag to carry purchases.
- Arrive early for the best selection.
- Carry cash since some vendors may not accept cards.
- Expect busiest times during summer/autumn harvests.
- Purchase baked goods, meats and dairy first before more delicate berries and vegetables.
- Look for unique products like flavored honeys, wild foraged jams, craft ciders.

The bustling, vibrant farmers' markets across the Cotswolds make for an immersive experience to witness first-hand the scope of fresh, locally-sourced produce. They encapsulate the efforts and passions of farmers, food producers and artisans who shape the landscape's bountiful harvests and time-honored goods. Visiting these markets lets you support the local food chain while sampling delicious products that provide an edible taste of the Cotswolds' culinary heritage.

Chapter 7

Shopping in the Cotswolds

- Antique Shops

With its old stone villages and stately country manors, the cotswolds is a haven for antique lovers. Its shops are brimming with treasures from past eras waiting to be uncovered. Here are some of the best:

Burford

Burford's steep high street is lined with antique shops offering everything from furniture to jewelry. Top picks include cotswold antique centre with three floors of merchandise like clocks and linens. Also browse in elizabethantony, the junk shop, and georgeedwards antiques for art, books, and collectibles. After shopping, recharge at one of burford's historic inns and tea rooms.

Stow-on-the-wold

As an important historic market town, stow is a focal point for antiquing in the cotswolds. Browse finds at upscale davidhanselmann antiques like mahogany bureaus and opulent glassware. Stop at wells market place antiques in a converted victorian corn warehouse for vintage home décor, from framed maps to oak dressers.

Tetbury

The upmarket town of tetbury hosts a nice selection of antique shops and vintage stores. Highlights include the house of dorchester, an impressive multi-level emporium perfect for losing yourself inside while admiring its mish-mash of antiques, art and collectibles. Vintage lives sells chic upcycled and painted furniture.

Moreton-in-marsh

Moreton's high street offers top antiquing stops like the semi-indoor moreton-in-marsh antiques centre with over 100 dealers. Chestnuts is packed floor-to-ceiling with retro treasures spanning furniture, glassware, books, artwork and ceramics. Cotswold country antiques has quality english and continental pieces.

Broadway

This picturesque village in the heart of the cotswolds contains many boutique antique shops. Find restored furniture, antique maps, prints and books at john r. derham antiques. John sheaf's vintage workshop sells upcycled vintage furniture curated with a modern eye. Broadway also has monthly antiques fairs from april to september.

Chipping campden

Browse the main street in this idyllic town to uncover antiques at reputable sellers like hick's antiques for art and jewelry and wickham house antiques, housed in a georgian townhouse stuffed with chandeliers and trunks. On the lower high street, yew tree house antiques is another great option.

Tips for antiquing in the cotswolds

- Chat with dealers to learn about eras, origins, and value of pieces that interest you. Their expertise is invaluable.
- Check items carefully for damage, repairs or replacements. Signs of age like patina add character.
- Be prepared to negotiate prices, especially for multiple purchases or high-ticket items.
- Ask about overseas shipping if you want purchases sent home. The shop may offer shipping services.
- If making a big investment, get pieces appraised independently.

For history buffs, antique-seekers, and collectors, browsing the myriad antique shops in the cotswolds' villages provides an exciting glimpse into british design, craftsmanship and material heritage. With luck and persistence, you may find that perfect well-preserved georgian table or piece of victorian jewelry to take home as a meaningful, lasting memento.

- Art Galleries

The Cotswolds art scene is thriving, with many galleries displaying works in a range of mediums by talented local artists. Here are some standout galleries to visit:

The Ox Barn, Chipping Campden

Housed in a meticulously converted 17th century barn, this acclaimed gallery exhibits British contemporary art in media including painting, ceramics, sculpture, and jewelry. Their rotating exhibitions feature established and emerging artists based in the Cotswolds. Don't miss their sculpture garden outside too.

Jillaroos, Gloucester

Jillaroos is an artist-run gallery focused on contemporary art by regional and U.K. talent. Mediums exhibited include painting, photography, mixed media, and jewelry crafted from silver, ceramics, and enamel. Exhibitions change monthly and spotlights are given to new artists.

The Rugby Gallery, Tewkesbury

Dedicated to British 20th century art, The Rugby Gallery maintains an extensive inventory of works spanning English landscape painting, maritime art, urban scenes, and still life. Artists represented include Alfred Wallis, William Scott, and John Skeaping. Consult their knowledgeable staff about works.

Museum in the Park, Stroud

Located within Stratford Park, this gallery has a diverse calendar of temporary exhibitions highlighting regional artists. Painting, sculpture, ceramics, textiles, and photography are some of the media showcased in the historic venue. The picturesque park makes for an ideal visit.

Bright Space Gallery, Stroud

Bright Space champions the best in contemporary art from Stroud-based artists and the surrounding area. The gallery's solo and group exhibitions encompass painting, printmaking, drawing, mosaic, and textile art. Visit their shop for art cards, jewelry, ceramics, and books too.

Jane Bordeleau Gallery, Slapton

The watercolor paintings of acclaimed local artist Jane Bordeleau are displayed in her light-filled gallery located on her family farm near the village of Slapton. Her realistic, emotive pieces depict Cotswold life, landscape, and architecture. Limited edition prints are available.

East Lodge Gallery, Tetbury

East Lodge is set within the Chavenage House estate near Tetbury. The modern gallery space exhibits diverse contemporary British art with a focus on emerging talent. Changing shows feature painting, sculpture, ceramics, mixed media, and jewelry.

Made by Hand, Winchcombe

This small gallery in Winchcombe has a curated selection of contemporary crafts by regional artists. Ceramics, textiles, wood carvings, glasswork, and jewelry are impressively displayed. Meet some of the actual makers during special studio open days.

Whether you're looking to browse or invest in art, the Cotswolds offers many excellent galleries that provide a platform for talented local artists. The variety and caliber of works displayed in these creative spaces, whether centuries-old barns or modern minimalist galleries, make for rewarding visits. Don't miss the opportunity to discover and connect with the Cotswolds' thriving contemporary art scene.

- Local Crafts and Souvenirs

The Cotswolds' charming villages offer plenty of places to shop for locally made crafts that make for ideal souvenirs and gifts. Look for these handicrafts during your visit:

Sheepskin and Leather Goods

Sheep grazing on the Cotswolds hills provide the prime material for leather crafts. Sheepskin rugs, leather-bound journals, and gloves are popular items. Talented leatherworkers like George McLaughlin in Stroud create bags and accessories. Leather is also used by Cotswoldssaddlemakers established in the 1800s like Lilliput Saddlery.

Wooden Items

Cotswolds woodcraft spans kitchenware, bowls, boxes, children's toys, jewelry and walking sticks intricately carved from local beech, oak and ash wood. Robert Opie makes puzzles inspired by regional scenery. Pick up hand-turned wood pens, décor objects and kitchen tools at the Farmers' markets.

Woolen Wearables

The Cotswolds is renowned for woolen goods like scarves, blankets, and knitwear. John Smedley knitwear factory in Lea has over 200 years of history. Other companies like Martingale

Handknits in Moreton-in-the-Marsh offer luxurious throws and accessories.

Ceramics and Pottery

Studios produce stellar ceramics from mugs to decorative wares. Emma Bridgewater in Stoke-on-Trent makes floral patterned pottery with Cotswolds motifs. The historic Royal Doulton Potteries are in Gloucester. Locally, Adam Frewer, John Hudson and Jim Malone are potters of repute.

Jewelry

Talented jewelers and silversmiths across the Cotswolds handcraft jewelry from classic to contemporary. Examples include Cotswold Designs in Bourton-on-the-Water for silver jewelry and Simon Gillespie in Stroud creating nature-inspired designs. John Taylor & Co in Loughborough dates back to 1760 crafting timepieces.

Food Products

Take home edible souvenirs made locally like fruit jams and marmalades, honey, cheeses, Cotswolds gin, craft beers and ciders. Seek out specialties like flavored ciders and meads at places like Cotswolds Distillery.

Soaps and Candles

Fragrant soaps, lotions and candles made with natural scents and ingredients like goats milk, beeswax and essential oils are lovely gifts. Cotswolds favorites include the Handmade Soap Company and Cotswold Fudge Company.

Prints and Paper Goods

Browse galleries and gift shops for scenic prints and paper products showcasing Cotswolds vistas, like notecards, guidebooks, maps and stationery. Carolyn Mitchell in Chipping Campden handcrafts marbled paper.

Walking Sticks

Cotswolds walking stick makers meticulously hand-carve sticks from local woods, with handles intricately shaped as sheep, duck heads or foxes. Robert Opie and T.W. Cook make custom sticks that make practical mementos.

From woolen garments, leather goods and pottery to foods that provide a taste of the landscape, specially crafted items sourced across the Cotswolds offer quality, locally made souvenirs. Peruse the traditional craft workshops and lively markets to find that memorable keepsake.

Chapter 8

Accommodation Options

- Cheltenham

Known for its Regency architecture, cultural festivals and gardens, Cheltenham is an elegant spa town that offers diverse lodging options. Choosing where to stay will depend on your interests and budget.

The Montpellier Chapter Hotel

For upscale boutique lodging, The Montpellier Chapter occupies a row of striking white Regency townhouses steps from Montpellier's upmarket shops and cafes. The chic rooms blend modern and Victorian flair with luxe amenities. Unwind at the stylish bar and restaurant overlooking Imperial Gardens.

The Bradley

The Bradley is a newly-built luxury hotel set on extensive manicured grounds just outside Cheltenham. Expect countryside views, sumptuous furnishings, a fine-dining restaurant, bar and indoor pool. The spacious, contemporary-styled rooms provide lavish comfort. It's perfect for special occasions.

Cowley Manor

Set within a historic manor house on 55 acres of parkland, Cowley Manor is a relaxing countryside retreat minutes from Cheltenham. The excellent spa, two restaurants, and luxuriously furnished rooms with quirky accents create a pampering escape. The Greenway Hotel next door offers similar charms.

The Wyastone

The Wyastone is a charming luxury hotel set within a 19th century estate surrounded by landscaped gardens. Inside you'll find country-chic rooms, a lounge with inglenook fireplace, lounge bar and conservatory. Outdoor pursuits like archery and fishing are also on offer.

Cheltenham Townhouse

This family-run Regency townhouse in Cheltenham's Pittville district provides friendly service and comfy rooms. Expect classic décor, complimentary breakfast, and a location near Pittville Park and the Pump Room. Rates are affordable given the high standards.

Ibis Cheltenham

For value chain accommodation, ibis Cheltenham is centrally situated near the train station and shopping area. The functional, contemporary rooms come with comfy beds, ensuite bathrooms and WiFi access. An onsite restaurant/bar and 24 hour front desk add convenience.

Portland House

This pleasing Georgian townhouse B&B has just three well-appointed rooms decorated in calming tones. Expect hospitable service, delicious breakfasts and a central but peaceful location near Imperial Gardens. Make reservations well in advance.

Cheltenham has accommodation to suit travelers whether you seek grand Regency hotels and country estates, cozy B&Bs, or value chain options. When choosing where to stay, factor in location – some neighborhoods like Montpellier and Pittville offer boutique shopping and architecture in walking distance. You're sure to find the ideal base to explore Cheltenham and the Cotswolds.

- Stow-on-the-Wold

With its charming market square and antique shops, Stow-on-the-Wold provides a quintessential Cotswolds base. From boutique hotels to traditional inns, these lodgings capture the essence of the town's beauty.

The Porch House

Dating back over 600 years, The Porch House is an ancient inn on Stow's main square. Expect exposed beams, a cozy bar with fireplace, and warmly decorated rooms filled with antique furnishings. Hearty breakfasts are served and dogs are welcome too.

Stow Lodge

This intimate hotel is set in an imposing 19th century Cotswolds stone house in central Stow. The chic, individually styled rooms feature plush fabrics, rainfall showers, and Nespresso machines. Unwind in the walled garden or by the log fire in the piano lounge.

Number Nine

Number Nine offers delightful bed and breakfast accommodation in a honey-hued townhouse near the market square. Its three rooms are tastefully decorated in neutral tones with luxury touches like Hypnos beds and monsoon showers. The cooked breakfasts are superb.

Kings Arms Inn

One of the oldest inns in Stow, parts of this charming property date back to the 14th century. Expect beamed ceilings, stone walls, and a warren of rooms and corridors. Basic rooms have period character along with modern bathrooms. The pub serves good ales and food.

St Edwards Lodge

This B&B occupies a 19th century rectory complete with stone mullion windows and oak doors surrounded by peaceful grounds. Its four elegant rooms come appointed with flatscreen TVs and tea facilities. The friendly owners serve an excellent breakfast too.

Treetops Cottage B&B

For a relaxing escape, this B&B sits in a secluded garden setting a 5 minute walk from town. The three traditionally furnished rooms come with garden views. Expect a warm welcome and superb breakfasts from the hospitable owners.

Stow has a wealth of atmospheric places to stay in properties of historic significance, from half-timbered medieval inns to Georgian manor houses. Many accommodate modern comforts while retaining a sense of the town's enduring charm and heritage. For the quintessential Cotswolds break, staying in accommodations with beamed ceilings, mullioned windows, and cozy nooks and fireplaces is a must.

- Burford

With its steep high street lined with stone buildings, Burford provides a picturesque base for exploring the Cotswolds. From boutique hotels to cozy B&Bs, these lodgings capture the town's old-world charm:

The Lamb Inn

This historic 17th century coaching inn on Sheep Street provides charmingly decorated rooms above a traditional pub. Expect sloping floors, beamed ceilings, and complimentary breakfast. The restaurant serves good locally-sourced food too. Ask for rooms in the newer garden wing for more space.

The Bay Tree

For refined luxury, The Bay Tree is a peaceful boutique hotel set in a 17th century house on Sheep Street. The elegant rooms feature handmade furniture, monsoon showers, and complimentary sherry. Unwind in the cozy bar and lounge or walled garden. Breakfasts are sublime.

Swan Hotel

This luxe boutique hotel comprises two historic buildings on the High Street connected by a glass atrium. Inside find a fancy restaurant,bar, spa, and individually styled rooms with bold fabrics and monsoon showers.Antique furnishings and period character abound.

Bull Hotel

Standing on Burford's main intersection, the Bull Hotel dates back to the 15th century. Inside find beamed ceilings, stone walls, and large, classically furnished rooms. Hearty breakfasts are included and the restaurant serves decent pub classics.

Angel House B&B

For a friendly stay, Angel House B&B provides a charming 16th century long house on the High Street. Its three traditionally styled rooms come with Ottoman beds and original fireplaces along with modern comforts. Breakfast features home-baked bread.

Tolsey House

This family-run B&B sits in a distinguished 17th century merchant's house overlooking the Tolsey Museum. Elegant rooms have canopy or four poster beds and antiques. The cooked breakfasts are excellent. Afternoon tea is complimentary.

Pilgrim House B&B

Pilgrim House is a Tudor townhouse turned B&B offering three stylishly decorated rooms with freestanding baths, complimentary cake and sherry. The central location is ideal for exploring while the owners provide a warm, helpful welcome.

For its unspoiled medieval charm combined with chic amenities, Burford provides the perfect Cotswolds retreat. Lodging in the honey

-colored stone buildings that line its sloping main street immerses you in the town's enduring antiquity, whether you opt for historic inns, posh boutique hotels or cozy B&Bs.

- Cottages and Country Inns

For a quintessential Cotswolds break, staying in a pastoral cottage or countryside inn lets you fully embrace the rural pleasures and natural beauty. These charming options abound:

Arlington Row Cottages, Bibury

These 17th century weavers' cottages overlooking Bibury Trout Farm and the River Coln are the most photographed Cotswolds dwellings. Choose from various sized cottages with exposed beams, stone walls and modern interiors for a fairytale stay.

Snowshill Hill Cottages, Snowshill

Escape to these two cottages atop Snowshill Hill that provide splendid views over the Cotswolds hills. The cottages blend rustic character like stone fireplaces with well-equipped kitchens and luxurious bathrooms for cosy, romantic stays.

Donnington Brewery Cottages, Stow-on-the-Wold

Situated on a working brewery estate dating to the 18th century, these six self-catering cottages have loads of character alongside smart interiors with wood burners and WiFi. The surrounding Donnington Valley is stunning.

The Painswick, Painswick

Originally an 18th century inn, The Painswick has been transformed into a luxe 16-room countryside hotel. The chic rooms, restaurant, and bar are complemented by an outdoor pool, spa hut, and immaculate gardens ideal for relaxing.

The Wheatsheaf Inn, Northleach

This 14th century coaching inn oozes charm with its exposed beams, stone walls, and homey décor. Alongside pub fare and ales, it offers cozy rooms filled with antiques and modern bathrooms for an atmospheric stay.

The Wild Rabbit Inn, Kingham

Expect the utmost Cotswolds coziness in this Michelin-starred restaurant and inn housed in a mellow 18th century building. Savor freshly sourced meals in the dining room with stone floors and roaring fire before retreating to the elegant rooms.

Foxhill Manor, Farncombe

For opulent countryside luxury, this manor house hotel set on a 450-acre estate features chic rooms, a farm-to-table restaurant, bar, and relaxing spa. Local activities like archery, fishing, and falconry are on offer alongside beautifully manicured grounds.

Whether tucked down a tiny lane in a sleepy village or perched on a hillside overlooking rolling fields, cottage and country inns encapsulate the essence of the Cotswolds' beauty. Their bucolic settings, beamed ceilings, and cozy interiors make coming home to them after a day of exploring particularly rewarding.

Chapter 9

Practical Information

- Weather and Best Time to Visit

Weather

The Cotswolds has a temperate climate influenced by the surrounding hilly terrain. Due to its inland location, it experiences warmer summers and colder winters than coastal areas of Britain.

Summer (June to August) sees average highs of 22°C and lows of 12°C though hot spells over 30°C occur. Expect sunny, warm days ideal for walking and exploring villages and gardens. Afternoons can be rainy.

Autumn (September to November) offers cool, crisp days with more rain as winter approaches. September still reaches 20°C while November highs average 10°C. Trees display vivid colors in October during fall foliage season.

Winters are chilly, with average highs of 7°C and lows dipping below freezing. December to February brings increased rainfall and possible snow or ice, especially in higher altitudes. Mist and fog are common. Short daylight hours limit exploration.

Spring (March to May) starts off cool but steadily warms up to average May highs of 16°C. Blooming daffodils, blossoms and lush green countryside make spring a beautiful time for hikes and garden visits. Afternoon showers are common though.

Best Time to Visit

Peak tourist season is May to September when the weather is sunniest and warmest. Expect crowds in popular towns and higher hotel rates.

March to May and September to November are ideal times with fewer visitors. September still offers sunny days to enjoy outdoor pursuits. Spring (especially May) provides a colorful display of blossoms and flowers.

Winters offer the least crowds and lowest rates but the cold, damp weather limits appeal for some. But wintry scenery has its own allure.

Major Festivals and Events

The Cotswolds' many fairs and festivals take place on particular dates annually. Notably:

- Cheltenham Literature Festival: October

- Stratford-upon-Avon Literary Festival: April-May
- Cheltenham Jazz Festival: April-May
- Stow Horse Fair: May
- Snowshill Manor Craft Demonstrations: Selected Sundays from April to October

Blockley Apple Festival: October

Visiting during these celebrations allows you to experience the region's culture and traditions at their liveliest and most vibrant.

The Cotswolds provides a delightful escape year-round. But planning your visit during the drier, warmer spring to fall months maximizes opportunities to explore its villages, outdoor trails, stately homes and colorful gardens. Whether you prefer peak or off-season travel, you're sure to be enchanted by the Cotswolds whatever the weather!

- Local Transportation

The Cotswolds covers a large rural area, so utilizing different modes of transportation is often necessary to get around. Here are the main options for traveling within the region:

Train

Rail service connects major Cotswolds towns and also provides access from London and other cities. Key stations include:

- Moreton-in-Marsh – On the Cotswold Line with regular direct trains to London Paddington, Oxford, Worcester.
- Charlbury – On the Cotswold Line, serving Burford, Woodstock, Kingham.
- Cheltenham – Direct trains to London Paddington, Bristol, Birmingham.
- Gloucester – Served by Great Western Railway trains to London Paddington, Cardiff, Bristol.
- Kemble – Serves Cirencester, links to London Paddington, Swindon, Stroud.

Bus

Local bus companies like Pulhams Coaches, Stagecoach, Swanbrook and Marchants run regular bus services connecting villages like Bourton-on-the-Water, Stow-on-the-Wold, Tetbury, Painswick. Useful routes include:

- #801 (Cheltenham to Bourton-on-the-Water via Stow)
- #855 (Cheltenham to Chipping Campden via Broadway)
- #W1 (Winchcombe to Cheltenham)

Key bus stations are Cheltenham Promenade, Bourton-on-the-Water George Moore Community Centre and Stow-on-the-Wold High Street.

Taxi

Taxis are available to book in major towns and villages. Good for short trips or when buses/trains aren't operating. Popular companies include:

- Mercury Taxis (Stow-on-the-Wold, Bourton-on-the-Water)
- Cotswold Taxis (Cirencester)
- AJC Cheltenham Taxi

Car Rental

Driving allows maximum flexibility for harder-to-reach villages. Rentals are available in Cheltenham, Gloucester, Swindon, Oxford from companies like Hertz, Enterprise, Europcar. Automatic cars are easiest for Cotswolds' narrow winding roads.

Bicycle

Cycling is a pleasurable way to travel between nearby villages. Rentals are available in Bibury, Bourton-on-the-Water, Broadway, Chipping Campden and other towns. Popular bicycle routes include the Thames Path and Windrush Way.

On Foot

The Cotswolds offers outstanding walking opportunities. Trails like the Cotswold Way, Wychavon Way, and Wardens Way allow you to hike between towns and soak up the rural scenery.

Boat

Take fun river cruises from Cirencester along the Thames to towns like Lechlade. Or board a Thames riverboat in Oxford travelling westwards through the Cotswolds water meadows.

Whether you opt for riding local buses, hiring a bike, driving a rental car or putting on your walking boots, it's easy to get around the Cotswolds using its various transportation options. Mix and match different modes to create your ideal travel experience. Seeing the breath-taking countryside as you journey between villages is part of the Cotswolds' unique charm.

Cotswolds:

Visitor Centers

The Cotswolds has several tourist information centers that provide useful maps, brochures, guidebooks and expert local knowledge about attractions, transportation, tours, accommodation and more. Some key visitor centers include:

- Bourton-on-the-Water – Centrally located in the village, helpful for exploring the Lower Slaughter villages.

- Burford – Resources on visiting Burford, Cirencester, Bibury, the Windrush Valley.

- Cirencester – Extensive info on the "Capital of the Cotswolds", Roman history, museums, markets.

- Cheltenham – Maps, guides, booking services focusing on Cheltenham's cultural offerings, shopping, dining.

- Stow-on-the-Wold – Broad range of Cotswolds information; walking routes, attractions, historic sites.

- Tetbury – Great for resources on Tetbury town, the Arts & Crafts movement, Highgrove House, Westonbirt Arboretum.

- Witney – Details on exploring Witney, Cogges Manor Farm, the River Windrush, OxfordshireCotswolds.

- Mobile VICs – Traveling information centers visit many smaller villages during peak season with guides.

Tip: Visitor centers provide free WiFi access for quick internet searches, route planning or ticket booking while touring the Cotswolds.

Safety Tips When Visiting the Cotswolds

- Use caution when driving on the narrow country roads. Pull over when possible if traffic is backing up behind you.

- Park only in proper designated car parks in villages. Don't leave valuables visible in your car.

- When hiking, always wear appropriate footwear and clothing for the trail conditions and weather. Carry water and snacks.

- Follow warning signs and stick to marked footpaths when walking through farm fields, woodland or meadows. Using public rights-of-way prevents trespassing on private property.

- Check online or with the local tourist office for footpath status. Trails may close periodically for maintenance or during lambing season.

- Apply sunscreen and wear hats on sunny days. The UK sun can still burn you even if temperatures feel mild compared to other destinations.

- Be prepared for afternoon rain showers even on clear mornings. Carry a small foldable rain poncho or jacket.

- Don't approach or feed livestock like cattle, sheep and horses you encounter in fields. Observe them from a distance.

- During winter, ice and snow can make paths slippery. Use hiking poles for added stability and wear boots with good traction.

By using common sense and following basic precautions, you can safely enjoy everything the Cotswolds countryside has to offer all year round. Stop by one of the area's many helpful visitor information centers to get oriented and educated before your trip.

Two Week Itineraries

Trying to fit everything into a 2 week trip to the Cotswolds can be daunting. These recommended 2 week itineraries help maximize your time:

Week 1: Western Cotswolds

Days 1-3: Base yourself in Cheltenham to explore Regency architecture, promenade, museums, dining and nightlife. Take a day trip to Broadway or Sudeley Castle.

Days 4-6: Stay in Lower Slaughter walking to Bourton-on-the-Water and Stow-on-the-Wold. Leisurely touring villages, gardens and Bibury on day trips.

Days 7-9: Stay in Burford to browse antiques and visit Cotswold Wildlife Park, Kelmscott Manor. Day trip possibilities are Oxford, Witney, Cirencester or the Swells villages.

Week 2: Northern and Eastern Cotswolds

Days 1-3: Stay in Chipping Campden and tour upper Cotswolds. Visit stately homes at Hidcote and Snowshill, quintessential villages like Broadway and Blockley, enjoy peaceful country walks.

Days 4-6: Base yourself in Stroud or Nailsworth for a more local artsy ambiance. Great farmers market, galleries, café culture, nearby Painswick and Slad Valley.

Days 7-9: Stay in Tetbury to peruse antique shops, Westonbirt Arboretum, Highgrove gardens tour. Also ideal for exploring Minchinhampton Common, Rodmarton Manor, Woodchester Mansion.

This provides a sampling of the most beautiful villages combined with key attractions across the Cotswolds regions. Adapt to suit your particular interests – add more days for hiking, gardens or stately homes as desired!

Two Week Best of the Cotswolds Itinerary

Immerse yourself in all of the Cotswolds' quintessential charms with this comprehensive 2 week itinerary:

Days 1-3: Cheltenham – Regency architecture, promenade, museums, dining

Day 4: Sudeley Castle, Winchcombe, Belas Knap neolithic tomb

Day 5: Broadway Tower, Snowshill, Broadway, Stanway villages

Day 6: Hidcote Manor Gardens

Day 7: Stratford-upon-Avon – Shakespeare attractions, Anne Hathaway's Cottage

Day 8: Bourton-on-the-Water, Lower Slaughter, Upper Slaughter

Day 9: Bibury trout farm, Arlington Row, Bourton Horse Fair (if scheduled)

Day 10: Stow-on-the-Wold market day, Cotswold Farm Park

Day 11: Moreton-in-Marsh, Chastleton House, Batsford Arboretum

Day 12: Burford, Cotswold Wildlife Park, Kelmscott Manor

Day 13: Tetbury shops, Westonbirt Arboretum, Highgrove House (tour)

Day 14: Painswick Rococo Garden, Woodchester Mansion, Rodmarton Manor

Day 15: Berkeley Castle, Dr. Jenner's House Museum, Edward Elgar birthplace museum

This covers all of the Cotswold region's must-see attractions and villages for a fulfilling two week vacation. Extend your stay or rearrange days as desired – you can't go wrong exploring any pocket of the enchanting Cotswolds!

Conclusion

With its unmatched villages, stately mansions, colorful gardens and sweeping countryside vistas, the Cotswolds offers idyllic English countryside at its finest. Follow winding country footpaths under stone arches, admire cloud-dotted hillsides, and find solace away from modern life in this quintessential rural landscape.

Each Cotswolds town and village has managed to retain its individual character and charm through the ages. Tour majestic Berkeley Castle, enjoy Low Slaughter's tranquil mills, and walk in the footsteps of Romans at Cirencester to experience the depth of history here.

The Cotswolds has also cultivated a flourishing local food scene. Treat yourself to farm-sourced meals at critically acclaimed restaurants and cozy pubs. Shop for produce at farmers markets overflowing with Cotswolds honey, cheese, fruit and vegetables.

As this guide has illustrated, the Cotswolds provides endless opportunities for exploration and inspiration. Its natural beauty, cultural richness and living heritage leave visitors beguiled. Whether you seek relaxation or adventure, pampering stays or countryside rambles, you're guaranteed to cherish your Cotswolds experience.

This table of contents provides a comprehensive overview of the topics covered in the Cotswolds travel guide. Let me know if you'd like to make any adjustments or if there's anything else you'd like to include.

NOTE

NOTE

NOTE

NOTE

NOTE

NOTE

NOTE

NOTE

NOTE

Made in the USA
Las Vegas, NV
03 October 2024

96233186R00105